NOT FOR QUEEN A

NOT FOR QUEEN AND COUNTRY

Edward Denmark

For my wife Tricia.
All my love.
Eddie.

Acknowledgements

Photographs are published with the kind permission of Crown Copyright, British Aerospace and Pacemaker International Ltd.

Foreword

Public interest in military matters is such that most bookshops have a section devoted to military affairs.

The range on offer varies from glossy coffee-table reference through anthologies of military writing to the biographies and autobiographies of famous commanders past and present. At least two shelves will be devoted to works concerning the *Special air services* some full of recycled fiction purporting to be fact, and others with dramatic titles that tell hair-raising stories – which the authorities back in Hereford would rather have remained untold. Presumably, it will not be long before the *SAS Book of Flower Arrangement, The Special Forces Guide to Origami and the SBS Manual of Underwater Basket Weaving* feature on some publishers list. The magic *SAS* acronym seems to sell books by the hundred-weight.

It is a genuine pleasure therefore to read the account of an ordinary soldier who has done some extraordinary things. Edward Denmark joined the Army in 1980 as a Gunner and specialised in missile anti-aircraft defence. In this role, he protected me and my teams at Ajax Bay Field Hospital, Falkland Islands, in 1982. I can recall with gratitude the flaming wreckage of an Argentine Air Force Skyhawk falling into San Carlos water on 25th May having received a Rapier missile from T Battery (Shah Sujah's) of 12 Regiment Royal

Artillery up its tailpipe. We were equally pleased to be able to treat the pilot's fractured knee following his successful, but very very low level ejection.

Edward Denmark went on to attempt parachute selection, which he failed due to illness, but which is reported honestly and directly here. This was followed by service in Northern Ireland which is also described with a vivid detail that makes it a genuine contribution to the often fanciful literature on that tortured province. The mainland British public is often reluctant to think too deeply on the subject of trouble over the water, but reading this will help to create more informed opinion – and perhaps make people realise that the freedoms they take for granted have been fought for in the past and are still worth fighting for now . . .

Rick Jolly OBE
Surgeon Captain RN (Retired)

1

"Who is a smart boy then!" cooed my parents. It was my first day at school and I still remember how proud I felt with my new togs on. This was no mean feat as I was one of ten children, with two brothers and seven sisters, and money was very hard to come by. Despite this, we were all clean, well dressed and looked after. I was closest to two of my sisters, Mary, who is one year younger, and Ali, who is a year older. The rest of my brothers and sisters were older and were either working or at high school. My father was an officer in the Merchant Navy and so was not home very often. It must have been a hard struggle for my mother trying to raise her brood. We lived in Moreton on the Wirral, a peninsula situated between the estuaries of the River Mersey and the River Dee looking out to the Irish Sea. At this time, in 1966, it was still classed as Cheshire, not becoming Merseyside until 1974.

Despite the lack of money, I still recall those early days with fondness: Days out to the beach, the smell of baking as my mother turned out tray after tray of cakes. Our home, sparse of any real furniture, was always kept clean and tidy. It must have been a losing battle with us all running around.

However, when I was about nine or ten years old things began to change for the worse. I was sent to school with my shoes unpolished, the odd rip in my trousers, odd socks on and my hair left uncut. My sister's appearance had taken a

I

turn for the worse as well. Because of my tender years, I never questioned why this was happening, but the other kids in school were quick to notice and as a result my two sisters and I began to get bullied. I was kicked and punched but it was the verbal abuse I hated the most, all the name calling. Life became very miserable indeed.

When I reached the age of twelve or thirteen, I began to fight back and, like bullies the world over who meet with some resistance, they left me alone in search of easier prey. But things at home got no better. The reason for our misery and scruffy turn out was now understandable to me even at my tender years. My mother was drinking – and drinking a lot.

At what stage she succumbed to the bottle I still don't know. By now my father had returned from sea for good and he was working in the local chocolate factory, Cadburys. Most of my sisters and two brothers had married and left home. It was around this time that I joined the local army cadet force. One of my friends had joined and seeing him in his uniform for the first time I knew I had to give it a go. He took me and my mate Mick along to one of the drill nights. I loved it; this was my oasis. I remember the night I picked my uniform up. There were ten of us stood around outside the regimental sergeant major's office. We had all joined within a few weeks of each other.

"YOU SHOWER GET IN HERE!" bellowed a voice from inside the office. We all squeezed in. The RSM was sitting behind his desk a plump man with a ruddy face. Out of the corner of his mouth hung a cigarette.

"We only have five uniforms to issue tonight," he said. My heart sank. "So the rest of you will just have to wait."

"Right! Get a two bob piece out of your pockets," shouted a sergeant who was standing in the corner. Three of those present didn't have one, so they were told to piss off. The odds were getting better. "Right, those who get heads get their uniforms, those who get tails wait," and he beamed "we will flip till we only have the five, so don't get too exited."

I flipped my coin and looked down, TAILS. Without a moments hesitation I turned the coin over. I felt the colour drain from my face. Had I been seen? No, but my hands were shaking. Only four of us got heads so we left the office while the tails flipped for last position. I did feel a bit guilty, but I got my uniform home, I put it straight on and ran down to the local chippy to try it out.

I had some wonderful times in the cadets going away for weekends and summer camps. Sitting in the cookhouse on one particular weekend in Altcar, near Southport, a few of the local territorial army walked in, their faces smeared in camouflage war paint, carrying huge machine guns. I stared in awe. These were the first real soldiers I had seen. That's what I want to be, I thought.

Life at home had become very miserable because of my mother's drinking, more so when she did not have the money to buy it. It was a rather odd situation because it was accepted that she drank. Coming home from school I never knew what would greet me as I came through the door. She would either be in a stupor or in a rage, depending on whether she had managed to buy drink or not.

As soon as I was old enough I left school. There was never any question of me staying on to sit my exams. I left school and I left home and went to live with my sister, Twink, in London. I had no plans, I just had to get away. I stayed in London for just over a year and I got a dead end job packing cat litter. I was never happy and in 1978 I returned home to Moreton. I got myself a job in Cadbury's where my father was working. Life at home was no better, but I now had my independence, which did make it easier.

My mind was still on the army, but I was afraid to commit myself. One day I would think 'just join' and the next I would think 'what if I don't like it'.

The one thing I was certain of was that I would not be staying at the chocolate factory. It was mind numbing and very tedious work indeed, and although it was a job and money, I hated it. Looking round at some of the men I used to think that will be me in thirty years. It sent a shiver down my spine. Some of the men looked well beyond their years.

During the summer of 1979, as the drink took its toll, my mother's health began to fail. She became bedridden and deteriorated as each day passed. It was heartbreaking to watch. I will never need to be told the dangers of alcohol because I have seen the most caring, funny person lose it all to the demon drink.

One hot sunny August afternoon I was in work. Amid the heat and noise of the factory my mind was elsewhere when I felt a tap on my shoulder. I spun round to be confronted by the foreman. He had a very serious look on his face.

"Your wanted over the surgery, son," he said.

"What for Bill?" I asked.

"Err, I don't know," he replied. "Off you go and don't worry about this lot," he shouted as I walked away. I knew what it was, but on reaching the surgery I was shocked to see my father sitting in a chair sobbing.

"Your mother has died," he spluttered. I knew it was coming and when it finally did I did not want to believe it. The next year passed in painful bouts of feeling sorry for myself. I was mixed up. Every one of the family changed, not just me. Things would never be the same. In the summer of 1980, at the age of 19, almost a year since losing my mother, I was walking home from work feeling fed up with myself when I looked back at the factory and I thought its now or never, if I don't join the army now I never will. My mind was made up.

As I was on the late shift the next day I decided to visit the local army careers office in Birkenhead. I told no one of my plans. The next morning I was up early, my father had already left for work. I was nervous. "What do I say when I get in the office?" I kept asking myself. My hair at the time was long and desperately needed cutting. I wore my duffel coat and training shoes. What a sight I must have looked.

I jumped on the bus to Birkenhead. It stopped just short of the army careers office in Borough Road. I got off and began the short walk. My stomach was in knots, my mind was racing I was so scared. I reached the office, and pulled the door. It would not open, Oh! God its closed I thought. "PUSH! . . ." screamed a voice. I pushed the door. It opened, I felt my face glowing. "I have blown it!" I thought.

I looked up to see the recruiting sergeant sitting behind his desk. He looked immaculate in his best uniform, his medal ribbons on his left breast, his boots gleaming under his desk. He had a scowl on his face. There were two other lads sitting on chairs to the left of me and both were giggling at my encounter with the door.

"Can I help you?" asked the sergeant.

"Yes, I want to join the Army." I replied.

"Well, you're in the right place," he said. "At least you got that right." The two lads burst out laughing. "Sit down," he offered. "What do you want to do in the army?" he asked.

"Be a soldier," I replied. He took a deep breath.

"I know you want to be a soldier, but have you thought what regiment or trade you would like?"

"The Scots Guards," I said. It was all I could think of at the time. I had seen them trooping the colour on the telly. "Well sunshine if you can get through basic training with them you are a better man than me!" he grinned.

"Right, get these filled in and then come back," he said, passing me a wad of forms after taking my details.

That was it, I had made the first move. On the way home, however, I did contemplate throwing the forms in the bin, but I went back the following day with my forms filled in, this time remembering which way the door opened. A week or so later I received a letter inviting me to sit an aptitude test. When I arrived at the careers office on the appointed morning, there were about seven other lads there already. We were shown into a small classroom to the rear of the office where we each sat behind a desk.

The exam papers were already laid out on the desks.

"You have ten minutes on each subject," said the sergeant. "The subjects are maths, English and logic puzzles. A total of thirty minutes. GO!" he shouted. We turned the papers over and began. The time was up in what seemed like five minutes. The exam over, we all waited to be called in to find out the results of our work. I was third in. "Sit down", beckoned the now familiar sergeant. Besides him sat a captain, looking equally smart with the three pips on each of his epaulettes.

"Well, Denmark, how do you think you have done?" asked the captain.

"Not very good on the maths, Sir, as for the rest, I don't know." I answered truthfully.

"Well, I will put you out of your misery," said the captain, "your maths is not very good and you won't be flying helicopters, but you have passed." I went home feeling very pleased with myself.

The medical I underwent the following week was very basic, to say the least, performed by an elderly white haired doctor who passed me fit to become a soldier. The cat was out of the bag. I told my father of my intentions. He was concerned that I was giving up a steady job, but when he realised that I was not going to be deterred he wished me luck. Some of my work mates thought I was a fool.

"What about going to Northern Ireland?" most asked.

"Not every soldier gets sent there," I would reply. The sergeant in the careers office had told me that!

The morning I was to take the oath of allegiance arrived and I was up with the larks. I caught the train to Liverpool, along with all the other commuters, wearing my best shirt and trousers, shoes polished. No-one took a blind bit of notice of me. They had their heads in their newspapers, some were even dozing.

Eventually, the train pulled in at St James station my stop. I felt a panic rise in me. The realisation of what I was about to do hit me. I left the station and crossed the road where the army careers office is situated, but I waited round the corner out of sight. I was not having second thoughts, but I needed to compose myself. Having done this I walked around the corner and straight in to the office pushing the door the right way.

"Yes, can I help you?" asked the sergeant. I explained why I was there. "Up the stairs, turn right, sit down outside the first office." When I arrived there were already two lads sitting there.

"Ay, mate, you're to take the oath?" one of them piped up.

"Yes," I said, "you too?"

"Yes" he replied. "What regiment ya goin' in?" he asked.

"I don't know yet why do you?" I asked.

"I'm goin' in the Paras for 22 years," he boasted.

"I only want to sign on for three years to see if I like it first." I said. At that moment a sergeant came walking down the corridor.

"Right you three, in here." he said, as he ushered us in to the office. "The Colonel has arrived, make sure you address him as Sir and stand up straight." The Colonel entered the office flanked by two junior officers. We were as stiff as brush handles.

"Stand easy gentlemen, relax!" barked one of the officers to make sure we understood.

7

"Gentlemen, please take that worried look off your faces, this is not supposed to be a solemn affair, its the start of your military careers," said the Colonel. After promising to defend Queen and country against all enemies, foreign and domestic, we were in. "Why did you want to join the army?" asked the colonel, looking at me and catching me unawares.

"I don't know" was all I could get out. He looked at me as if to say 'you poor misguided bastard.'

"Yes, well, very good." The sergeant standing behind him, his face red, just stared at me. I wasn't sure if he was trying to suppress his laughter or if he was angry at me. The colonel then rounded on the guy next to me. "Why do you want to join the army?"

"Because my uncle is in the Royal Signals and I want to follow in his foot steps," answered the smart arse.

"And you?" said the colonel, asking the lad standing next to 'smart arse'. He had obviously taken his cue because he repeated him parrot fashion. This was all too much for the sergeant. He burst out laughing much to the dismay of the officers.

Walking out of the careers office, I felt so excited looking at the posters on the walls of soldiers skiing, absailing and walking on sunsoaked beaches. 'I have made the right decision,' I thought to myself.

I was told to report to a barracks at Sutton Coldfield near Birmingham on the 6th of June, 1980. I had a list of articles to take with me ranging from toothbrush to writing paper. The barracks was a dispersal point. We would all undergo more written tests and, depending on the grade achieved and if there was a vacancy, you would be sent to the regiment of your choice. One did not need to be highly intelligent to get into the army, but what they did with you once you were in was another matter.

The day for my departure arrived. I was up early, but strangely I was no longer afraid. I knew there was no turning back. I had said all my goodbyes and I was given a nice writing set by work mates. I had already begun to start fitness training some weeks before in preparation. I picked up my one small bag and walked out of the door into my new life, a life I knew nothing about yet!

2

I boarded the train at Liverpool's busy Lime Street station.

"This is the right train for Birmingham?" I asked an old lady sitting by the door.

"Oh yes," she replied. The train was packed, but I eventually found myself a seat in amongst a group of other lads who I assumed were also going to join up. I spotted the lad from the careers office. He was giving another lad his expert views on the Paras. As we sat there waiting for the train to pull out of the station, I considered jumping off and going home, but I knew in my heart it wasn't a real option, I was in too deep now. There were quite a few of us going to Sutton Coldfield and some of the lads had taken the trouble to get haircuts in anticipation. I was sorry I hadn't because I looked like I had been dragged through a hedge backwards. We all eyed each other with suspicion, but already the different characters were beginning to show. Most like me chose to stay quiet, but one lad was gobbing off to all who would listen how hard he was, and that for him basic training was going to be a laugh. I took this act of bravado for what it was – 'bullshit'!

The train pulled in at Birmingham's New Street station and we all piled off like sheep following each other. Strangely, no one was talking now, even the lad who had been gobbing off had fallen silent. I couldn't believe how much luggage some of them had with them. One lad had no less than five suitcases. 'If he gets them up the stairs basic training will be easy enough,' I thought. I felt rather stupid having only a little bag with a change of clothes and a few of the items we were told to bring with us. We were greeted on the platform by a blackboard instructing us to present ourselves at a white bus outside the station.

At this point I kept telling myself that I had made a stupid mistake and if I had thought my Dad wouldn't have blown his top I would have got the next train home. We handed our documents to the corporal waiting by the white bus.

"Find a seat and keep quiet," he said without any expression. We had been sat there for around five minutes when the lad with the five suitcases emerged from the station. He was bright red and dripping in sweat. A snigger went round the bus and I thanked God it wasn't me they were laughing at. "Well who the fuck are you?" shouted the corporal. "Sherpa fucking Tensing!" We all laughed until the corporal turned round and told us to shut up. He then turned his attention back to suitcases. "How long do you think you will be staying in the army for sunshine?" he asked him.

"About three years," he replied.

"Three fucking years!" the corporal shouted back. "You've got enough luggage to last you twenty three fucking years, you idiot!"

"Sorry, Sergeant" replied Suitcases.

"FUCKING SERGEANT!" screamed the Corporal, "look at my arm you bloody half- wit. I am a corporal! Now get on the bus, before I lose my temper." No one lifted a finger to help Suitcases, including me because we were all scared of being tarred with the same brush. It felt safer to stay in the background unnoticed. After a short journey we arrived at the barracks, and although it was not an operational barracks as such it was far more modern than I had imagined it would be. We were all shown to our accommodation and then taken to the cookhouse for lunch. Even the food was enjoyable and we were able to eat as much as we liked.

Later that day we sat yet another written test and were told we would be informed of the results the following day. That night we were free to go to the NAAFI bar with a warning not to get too drunk. There were two soldiers in the bar when I arrived, with a group of potential recruits gathered around them listening to them recounting stories from Northern Ireland. I joined the other recruits and it was fascinating listening to their stories of killing terrorists. They had killed at least five each. Every so often they would bring proceedings to a halt to point to one of the assembled crowd and say, "Your round," and the chosen one would run to the bar and fetch them more beer. I was praying they didn't pick me as I didn't have much money and, fortunately they never did. After the bar had closed, they brought the evening to an end and both staggered off giggling. The irony of it was we all believed their bullshit and it made us even more determined to become soldiers They would have been better employed in a recruiting office.

The following morning we were out of bed early. This was the day we would find out if we would be going to our chosen regiments which would depend on the grades we had achieved and whether or not there was a vacancy in that particular regiment. After breakfast we were assembled in a large hall to wait for our results and a final interview. After waiting for two hours my name was called.

"Go in and stand to attention," said a sergeant ushering me into an office where a captain was sitting behind a desk.

"Sit down Denmark," he said without looking up. He was reading a file with my name written across it. Finally he looked up. "Okay" he said "you want to enlist into the er . . .

"Scots Guards, Sir" I said prompting him.

NOT FOR QUEEN AND COUNTRY

"Ahh, yes, the Scots Guards," he replied. "Well, I am afraid there are no vacancies at the moment." Before I could reply he added "Have you considered any other regiments at all?"

"No Sir," was all I could mutter. I just hadn't anticipated this. "Well, I am sorry," said the captain, "but I am afraid that is the situation at the moment. Have you heard of the Royal Artillery?" he asked.

"Yes sir" I replied.

"Well," he said, "let me tell you that the Royal Artillery is one of the finest regiments in the British Army and had there been a vacancy when I joined the army, that's what I would have gone into." My mind was racing to find an answer. 'The bloody Royal Artillery, I thought, what should I do?' As if reading my mind the officer cut in.

"The only alternative is if you go back home and we send for you when a vacancy comes up. But," he added, "I can't say how long that would be."

"I will be a laughing stock if I return home so soon' I thought, 'and my Dad had warned me not to give up my job.'

"Okay, Sir," I blurted out, "I will go into the Royal Artillery."

"Good lad," he said "you have made the right choice." That was it, the destination of my life was decided in a moment in that office.

The interviews over we were marched in a fashion over to the barber's shop for haircuts. I watched in sadness as the barber shaved the last signs of my past civilian life off my head. That night in our accommodation block we all talked of what regiment we were going to and it turned out that the captain had pulled the same stunt on a few of us. "That's a fine regiment and that's the one I would have gone into had there been vacancies at the time," he had told one lad about the infantry! The following day we were taken back to the same hall, but this time there was a number of desks laid out with the names of various regiments pinned on the front: Military Police, Royal Engineers, Royal Artillery. Sat behind each desk was a soldier with a pile of brown envelopes in front of him. We were called out in turn and each given an envelope with our reporting instructions and travel warrants inside. I was to report to Woolwich, south east London, the training depot of the Royal Artillery. All of the lads who were going to Woolwich gathered together and, luckily, one of the lads was from London and knew his way round. After dinner we were driven back to New Street station to catch the train for Woolwich. After a trek across London, we arrived at Woolwich station . Once again we were met by a blackboard instructing us to report to a minibus outside the station. As we made our way up the steps a voice boomed down to us.

"GET A FUCKING MOVE ON!" I looked up to see a sergeant standing there in his best uniform. I couldn't see his eyes under the gleaming peak of his cap. He carried a black, silver tipped cane which he tapped on the concrete floor. "Into the minibus and keep quiet you twats!" he yelled as we reached him. We quickly piled into the bus and drove the short distance to the barracks in silence. The sergeant speaking to the driver didn't say a word to any of us. On reaching the barracks a sentry raised the barrier and we drove in. This was different to the last barracks, very different. The place was immaculate, even the old gun outside the guardroom, (which I learned later, was a twenty-five pounder) was gleaming, with every inch of brass shining and the rope wrapped around its barrel blancoed white. Soldiers marched in perfect formations, no one ambled. A shiver ran down my spine as I realised that this was the real army.

The minibus pulled up outside a transit accommodation block. We were ushered out and taken to a room which was already occupied by some lads who told us that they had been there for three weeks and we were the last ones in. The following day we were paraded outside the block and a sergeant and two bombardiers appeared.

"Right, shut the fuck up and listen in!" shouted the sergeant. "I am Sergeant Jones and these two gentleman standing by me are bombardiers Price and Newman. You will address us as 'Staff' from this moment on and there will be no exceptions. Anyone failing to do this will be punished. Do you all understand?"

"Yes, Staff," we all shouted back.

"Right," he said, "it is our job to turn you people from layabouts into soldiers and make no mistake, that is what we are going to do. To that end the holiday is over and you will move over to Le Cateau Troop today. Your basic training will begin on Monday morning early!"

Later on that day we were issued our uniforms and equipment, which was referred to as our '1157', its Army serial number. I couldn't believe how much kit we had been given and I didn't know what most of it was for, despite my time with the cadet force. I soon realised that we were regarded as scum by all. Even the recruits who were only three weeks ahead of us looked down on us. There was a pecking order in place and it was taken seriously. We were at the bottom.

So it began. Le Cateau troop was made up of ninety-six recruits divided into three sections of thirty-two men. Each section occupied a floor of the training block. There were four rooms to a section and eight men to a room. Regardless of past military training, we started from scratch and it was painful because we were raw. We had been warned by another recruit who was some weeks ahead of us and kind enough to lower himself by speaking to us, that the lack of sleep was the hardest part of it and he was right because I felt creased within the first days. We began to learn the very basics of soldiering from marching (drill), how to strip a machine gun and a rifle (skill at arms), map reading, field craft and even military terminology. It was baffling at best. The discipline was harsh and adjusting was by far the hardest thing to do.

Any mistakes, no matter how slight, would bring the most brutal punishment. A wrong drill movement would, for example, warrant a crack over the head from the drill sergeant's pace stick. The pace sticks were heavy wooded instruments capped with brass, and the noise it made as it was brought down on some unfortunate recruit's head was sickening. I saw one lad take the full impact of a pace stick that was thrown at him and it knocked him out cold. The instructor, however, was more concerned that his pace stick was not damaged. The parade ground at Woolwich is huge and we would march up and down well into the night. Often the instructors would march us through the magnificent white gates called the South Arch back and into the barracks as though we had finished drill, only to 'about turn' us and take us back onto the parade ground.

We had what the army refers to as bullshit! Nothing was left untouched by it. The name of the game with bullshit is uniformity and this is what took up most of our precious hours and deprived us of much needed sleep. Our lockers for instance had to be set out in an identical way right down to the last inch. Our shirts and jumpers, even socks and under-pants, had to have the appearance of perfect square shaped boxes when viewed from the front. This was achieved by measuring and cutting cardboard and then pinning it inside the garments. Even our shoe polish tins had to be scraped off to reveal the shiny metal underneath. Our sheets and blankets had to be folded into a perfect square (bed block). All this would be measured by the staff and if the measure-ments were incorrect or they found a speck of dust or anything out of place the whole display would be thrown out of the window. It was soul destroying to watch many hours of hard work wrecked in a moment.

The punishment that followed was even worse, because the offender would be sent to the guardroom for a beating. This involved sit-ups, press ups and being run around to the point of collapse. But far worse was changing parades. This meant being given minutes to return back to the guardroom wearing various combinations of kit which could be anything from just underpants and boots to best uniform and a respirator (gas mask). This punishment was a killer because the staff enjoyed it and tried to outdo each other as to who could think up the most bizarre combination of clothing. This would go on for hour after hour, until the instructors grew bored with it and the the offender would have the laborious task of rebuilding his locker layout from scratch. To save ourselves time some of us would resort to sleeping on a blanket at the side of the bed to save having to rebuild the bed blocks each morning, but the staff got wind of it and warned us that if they caught us we could expect no mercy. They viewed it as cheating. I thought it was using our initiative.

As the long, hot summer months went by we became more efficient and began to think like soldiers, but the better we became the harder the staff treated us. We would drill all morning and go for back breaking runs in the afternoon, often returning to find the staff had trashed the rooms in our absence. We would return to find our locker layouts pulled out and scattered around the room and soap powder and water thrown about to make the cleaning up job that bit harder. It was all designed to break our spirits and it worked on some of the lads who applied for discharges. Others didn't even bother with that, simply slipping over the wall during the night, never to be seen again. I considered leaving myself on a few occasions, but the thought of all the people back home, who had never tried this, taking the piss out of me for failing spurred me on.

Physically, they pushed us to our limits. Opposite the main gates of the barracks was a wooded area called the Dell. This was where the assault course was situated along with three dirty smelling and stagnant pits full of green slimy water. After we had been round the assault course endless times and we were fit to drop we would then be ordered to leap into one of these pits and make for the opposite bank. Inevitably we would never do it fast enough so the staff would keep us there until they were satisfied that we were trying. It took many hours trying to wash the green slime from our clothes and restore the highly glossed finish to our boots.

Of all the physical training, I hated the gym sessions the most, because they were so disciplined. One of the Staff would stand in the centre of the gym with a whistle in his mouth and, depending on how many blasts he gave, we would carry out various exercises, forward rolls, sit ups and sprints. It was hard to keep count and we would often make mistakes and do the wrong exercise. The punishment for this was to be put in the horse box for the rest of the session but, contrary to what the staff thought, we enjoyed it, peeping through the slits, watching the other lads running around sweating buckets. One day there was four of us squeezed into the tiny space when one of the lads developed cramp, he fought between his fear of the Staff and the intense pain of his cramp. Finally the cramp won and he shot up with a howl, knocking the top of the horse box with his head.

"And who the fuck are you?" shouted one of the Staff, "Jack in the box?"

"Sorry, Staff" the lad pleaded, as we all sniggered at his misfortune.

The Staff were very clever at making money from us. One of their scams was to rent us a television, with each of us making a contribution of a couple of pounds per week. However, we worked it out that they were making enough out of us to buy a new telly each week! We said nothing because they would allow us the odd hour to watch it. They had to justify the money they made. As we progressed through the various stages of training, so our standing in the pecking order became higher. We were no longer the new recruits, because other troops had started their basic training. We all began to assume an arrogance in front of the new boys, though if any of the Staff were around they would bring us back to earth with a bang by reminding us that we hadn't even got to our regiments proper.

The physical training was very demanding even in the latter stages. I enjoyed the running, but it never ceased to amaze me that some of the lads would begin to struggle after a short distance. The physical training instructors who always accompanied us on these runs lost no time in showing the stragglers the error of their ways with a well aimed boot up the arse. The more I got to know the lads I was in training with, the more I began to think that some of them did not fit the image of what I thought soldiers should be like. I realised that it takes all sorts, but some of these lads hated it and even admitted that they had only joined the army because they couldn't get a job anywhere else. I felt sorry for them because I was now starting to like it more and more, so I made more of an effort and it got easier.

I only made one serious mistake and that was in skill at arms, where we were having a lesson on the light machine gun (LMG). It was a dry lesson, meaning that the weapon was not loaded, but even so we were taught from the very beginning that *all* weapons were to be handled as though they were loaded and with extreme caution. For some stupid reason after going through the drill correctly and bringing the working parts to the rear for inspection I touched the trigger and in effect fired the weapon. This is a very serious offence and is looked upon as a negligent discharge (ND). To make matters worse I smiled. Only out of nerves, but I smiled. With the grin still on my face, I felt what I can only describe as an explosion in my head and a pain so severe that it went through my body like a bolt of lightning. All I could see were a million stars. My next recollection was of being dragged to my feet and one of the Staff bawling in my face. I couldn't hear a word he was saying. Either I was too shocked or the smack around the head had sent me into a temporary deafness. I was thrown out of the classroom by the scruff of my neck were I remained till the lesson had finished. When all the others marched off I was taken inside for what I thought was going to be a good hiding. So scared was I standing outside the classroom, that I really did contemplate running off, but I reasoned that it would be a lot worse when I was caught. The staff member who had knocked me into next year took me through the weapons drill half a dozen times which I did without a hitch.

"You know how to do it," he said, "so do you know why I hit you?"

"For getting it wrong, Staff," I said.

"No, not for getting it wrong," he replied, "for fucking thinking it was funny."

"Sorry, Staff," I said.

"I hope you have learned your lesson. These weapons are not fucking toys and this is not a game."

"Yes, Staff," I replied.

"Right. End of the matter," he said, "go and rejoin the troop." I had certainly learned my lesson and I never forgot the Staff's words.

A few weeks before our pass out parade we were marched into our troop office and told by the Staff which regiment of the Royal Artillery we would be going to, what kind of weapons they used and what their particular role was within the army. I was to be posted to the 12 Air Defence Regiment who were based in Dortmund, Germany.

"As the name suggests," said the Staff, "12 regiment are an anti-aircraft regiment and they use a missile system called Rapier." I was none the wiser. "So, Denmark, you are to be a cloudpuncher." This was the first time I had heard that expression, but it was not to be the last. Any regiment that uses ground to air weapons is referred to as cloud-punchers.

In the October of 1980, the day of my passing out parade arrived. It was a wonderful day. I was so proud that I had made the grade and I knew that there have been people back home saying 'I told you he wouldn't do it' if I had failed. Now I could return home with my head held high.

Two weeks leave followed my passing out parade and instantly I noticed that I had grown apart from my mates. They showed no interest in me passing out and being posted to my first real regiment, but I put it down to the fact that I had now started a life which they knew nothing about.

My leave over, I reported back to Woolwich and the following day I flew to Dusseldorf airport in Germany. This was the first time that I had ever been abroad and whilst I was excited, I was also apprehensive about arriving at 12 Air Defence Regiment. I had heard all kinds of stories about the initiation ceremonies, that the NIGS (new intake gunner) or those just new in Germany would receive. There were only two other soldiers on the white bus with whom I had been in basic training. The others had gone to their various regiments.

We were met at the guardroom and taken to our batteries. I was the only one going to 'T' Battery, the other two were taken to a sister battery. The soldier escorting me walked two steps ahead and said nothing as I struggled to keep up with my luggage. Arriving at the barracks, made up from old Gothic buildings, I was shown to my room and told I would be sharing with three other lads. My escort warned me about one of them and told me not to lend him any money.

"In fact," he added "don't leave any valuables lying around, because he'll have them away!"

"Well, where are they all?" I asked.

"I'll show you" he said, and after securing my luggage away

in a locker and getting my bedding, he led me down some steps into the basement of the block. I wondered if he was setting me up for some cruel welcoming party as we reached the door. I could hear a racket coming from below. I pushed it open to be met by the sight of a dozen soldiers sprawled all over the bar, well and truly pissed. I had a drink pushed into my hand and was welcomed to 'T' Battery. The weekend passed in a drunken haze.

On the Monday morning I reported to my troop commander for my official interview. My uniform was immaculate with razor-sharp creases and the toe caps on my boots shone like mirrors. I tapped on to his office door.

"Come in," beckoned a voice from within. I marched in, stood to attention and saluted

"Gunner Denmark, sir," I said.

"Stand at ease, Gunner Denmark", he ordered and then he welcomed me to the battery. "I am a second lieutenant," he said, "and I am in charge of you and your welfare. If you have any problems do not hesitate to come and see me. Okay?"

"Yes," I replied. Second Lieutenant Andrews looked more like a smart version of a university drop-out (which it later turned out he was) with his glasses and boyish looks. He asked me a lot of questions about my background and family and even why I had decided to join the army. In fact, he showed a genuine interest in my welfare and genuinely made me feel welcome. I liked him immediately and as I was to find out he was a very good officer. Lt. Andrews went on to explain the make up of 12 Air Defence Regiment and 'T' Battery as a whole. 12 Air Defence Regiment had four batteries and each had four troops. Each troop had four rapier missile launchers, with the exception of the troop at headquarters. 'T' Battery had a total of twelve rapiers and was called Shah Sujah's because it had been raised many moons ago in the first Afghan war. It was, in name only, part of the Royal Horse Artillery. Andrews told me that I would be starting a signals course the following week and would then begin my rapier operator's course shortly afterwards. The duration of both courses would be seven weeks.

3

I settled in well with G troop of T Battery but there was also a pecking order here, and after my climb up the ladder while in basic training, I was now back at the bottom again. I completed my signals course and failed miserably along with a few of the other NIGs. I simply had no understanding of military communications and radios. I was bitterly disappointed and I took a lot of piss- taking from the other lads or sweats as the experienced soldiers were called. I passed the signals course eventually, but my opportunity to redeem myself came when I started my rapier course a few weeks later. I liked the rapier from the moment I set eyes on it. The rapier was an odd looking piece of kit, but as was proved in the Falklands war, it is a very lethal anti aircraft weapons system. It is easy to operate and providing the operator has a steady hand and a good eye, he is very capable of blasting the most modern multi million pound jet fighter from the skies with little effort. I enjoyed working on this astonishing weapons system very much and as result I passed with flying colours.

After my course I became a crew member on one of the rapiers, call sign 31D. The rapier was crewed by five men who were Sergeant Stewart Burton (Commander), Bombardier 'Geordie' Henwood, Gunner Tony Wilson (nicknamed Squirm for reasons I was to find out later), Rob Green

(who I had christened Chimp because of his gait which stuck)
and myself. Chimp had arrived a few weeks after me so we
were both still bottom-of-the-ladder NIGS and as a result we
were given all the crap jobs. I liked all the lads of our crew.
Stewart Burton had a well deserved reputation for not
suffering fools lightly and some of the lads were a little scared
of him. Not long after my arrival to the regiment, I saw him
dispatch another soldier who also had a reputation for being
hard. The soldier who had been drinking decided he would
settle the score of a previous argument and unfortunately the
pair of them clashed in my room as I lay there in bed too
frightened to move. After Stewart had knocked the other
soldier out, he walked away leaving him slumped onto my
bed covered in blood. I didn't know what to do in case he
woke up and set about me. Thankfully some of the sweats
came in and dragged the man out.

"Is this a regular thing?" I asked them in shock.

"It can be," one of them replied with a smile. Geordie
Henwood was very level headed and known as 'Army Barmy'.
He loved being a soldier which was in his blood. He was also
a workaholic and could not figure out why his colleagues were
not the same. His only weakness was his passion for tea. He
craved it like a drug addict craves for his next fix, but when
the chips were down Geordie was the man to have with you.
Squirm was a real Cockney character and as far as he was
concerned if a person was not born within the sound of the
Bow bells they were second class citizens. Squirm's passion
was West Ham Football Club and no matter what the subject
being discussed was he would somehow lead the conversation
back to the Hammers. Chimp, like me, was a new boy, but
whereas I would get pissed off because we had to do all the
crap jobs, Chimp laughed it off. This was soon noticed and
he began to get more than his fair share. He was also taken
advantage of by some of the more shady members of the
troop who borrowed money off him! But even the Chimp

soon realised that any weakness would be exploited and he wised up.

I made some good mates, one of them being Tony McColl (Mac) who hailed from Barrow-in-Furness where my own father was born and raised. Mac was in another troop but because of our link with Barrow in Furness we got chatting and soon became best mates. I have never met anyone with such a good sense of humour as Mac. He could take the piss out of anyone and anything including himself, but his sense of humour was frowned upon by some of the senior soldiers of the Battery, mainly because they lacked the wit to match him.

I tried to keep my nose clean and impress my troop sergeant major and troop commander. I was generally successful, apart from on one occasion where I was to learn the real reason why Tony Wilson was called Squirm. He persuaded me to go across to his room with him one morning, leaving the compound where we had been working. I was reluctant, because I knew, being the new boy, it would not go down too well if we were caught. Squirm eventually talked me round and we sat in his room drinking coffee which he was telling me about his tour of Northern Ireland from which 12 Regiment had just returned and I had just missed! It was nice to be sitting in the warm skiving. 'I could get used to this,' I thought. We had just finished our coffee and Squirm went to put the cups back in his locker. It was situated away from the wall and so when the door swung open and one of our Fijian sergeants appeared, he was out of sight. I had heard terrible stories about this man's temper and I was now wishing I had listened to them. "WHY THE FUCK YOU IN ERE!" he shouted. I was so frightened by what I knew was most certainly coming my way I just blubbered

"I don't know, Sergeant."

"YOU DON'T FUCKIN' KNOW?" he screamed even louder. "I tell you why you 'ere," he said, "because you a fuckin' skiver," and with that he stepped forward and gave me a smack across the head that made my eyes water. "Now back to work, you bastard!" he yelled, and as I passed him he gave me another smack on the back of the head for good measure. I ran back to the compound as fast as I could, feeling quite sure that I was now in the shit and most certainly in for another hiding when the sergeant told my commander, Stewart Burton. But he never did and in fact the Fijian sergeant came over to the compound a little later on and never mentioned the incident. I kept quiet about it myself until Squirm turned up. "Fuck me," he said, "that was close, I nearly got caught myself laughing at you, Scouse! The fucking noise when he whacked you!" he said, laughing. I declined anymore offers to skive with Squirm after that, but in all fairness he was a good soldier.

I liked being based in Germany. Whether it was because I had never travelled before or the culture was new to me, I don't know. A lot of the single lads had steady girlfriends and lived out of the barracks, spending most of their time living in and amongst the German population. Although officially it wasn't allowed the army seemed to turn a blind eye, but a number of these lads were so wrapped up in the German way of life that they even resented coming into work and would get away back to their girlfriends as soon as possible. Whenever I went out the same faces were always in the bars getting drunk. I even suspected that some of the older sweats were in the advance stages of alcoholism, but the army did not seem to bother. The only time it came to their attention was when someone failed to turn up for parade. I could see how easy it would be to fall in to that way of life. Everyone's existence seemed to revolve around getting pissed, a fact assisted by beer being so cheap it was practically given away.

I was saved from the perils of becoming a drunk in Germany in the summer of 1981, when 12 regiment moved lock, stock and barrel to Rapier Barracks on the outskirts of a small village called Kirton in Lindsey, near Scunthorpe. It must have been a great culture shock to the old sweats after the cosmopolitan hustle and bustle of Dortmund. Kirton in Lindsey consisted of a cluster of houses, a few pubs and a bank that opened every other day . . . and the beer was expensive! I was happy about the move because it meant that I would now be able to go home each weekend when not on duty. The only attraction for the drinkers was the bright lights of Scunthorpe and in particular a faded old club called Tiffany's. For some of the lads this seemed to be the centre of their world.

12 Regiment eventually fell in line with the sleepy pace of Kirton. All we seemed to do was sweep up and clean vehicles and take part in the odd exercise in the Otterburn area. Life became boring and as a result of the boredom the lads started to look for mischief and things to keep themselves amused. For one group the source of their amusement was a lad who shared my room called Robin. Robin was overweight for a soldier and he also told some stupid lies in a vain attempt to win friends, but he was harmless and very vunerable. He was perfect bait and the lads just took the piss out of him and used him as a lap dog. Though he was an ardent Preston North End football fan he even changed his allegiance to West Ham in a bid to win favour. It didn't work.

One night Robin was invited over to the home of one of the group who was married and living in army quarters on the pretence that they were having a small fancy dress party. All this was concocted with the full consent of the soldier's wife. I had given up trying to tell Robin that he was being taken for a ride, he would not listen. So off he went to the party, just over the road from the barracks, like a lamb to the slaughter. That was the last I saw of Robin until just after midnight when I was awoken by his figure standing in the doorway crying.

"Robin, what the fuck's up?" I asked reaching up to turn my bedside lamp on.

"Look what they have done," he said, pointing to his now bald head and then he went on to tell me the full story. After he had arrived at the house and had a few drinks, Robin was taken upstairs and given his fancy dress which was a pair of stockings and suspenders and a pair of knickers. He was encouraged to get dressed up by the other lads, themselves wearing an array of women's underwear, but after shaving his head they threw him out into the street. They then informed the guardroom that there was a pervert stealing knickers from washing lines. He somehow made it back to the room, minus his underwear. Robin decided to run away after this episode, but like all deserters he was eventually caught and sent to a military prison for his troubles. Poor Robin got a very rough deal from the army, though he brought most of it upon himself.

I went home almost every weekend. Such was the boring pace of life in Kirton that going home was all I looked forward to during the week. It was during one of my weekend visits home that tragedy struck. I had gone to a remote field at the back of my father's house with a friend of mine who owned a small motorbike. It was a quiet Sunday afternoon and I intended spending a few hours riding the bike around the field until I caught my train back to the barracks later in the evening. I was sat on a small hill overlooking the field watching my mate buzzing around while I waited for my turn. After a while two other lads turned up, each with a bike of their own. The younger of the two lads, who was no more than fourteen years old, rode up the hill towards me. We had a few words about my mate's bike before he rode off again and carried on riding around the field for a while.

A bit later on, however, I watched as these two lads rode across the field towards each other. Only the older lad was wearing a crash helmet! At first I felt no concern because it was a wide open field with plenty of room. Soon, however, I felt a sense of panic because neither of them was turning away and they were very close. I expected one of them to turn away at the last moment but they collided with a sickening thud. For a second I could not believe what I had just witnessed. As I ran down the hill towards the pair, I saw the younger one leap to his feet and stagger a few feet before collapsing again into the long grass. The older of the two lads was also in serious trouble because he still had his motorbike on top of him and the engine was still running. I pulled the motorbike from him shouting for my mate to go for help. The lad had some very bad cuts to his legs and more seriously he had swallowed his tongue. As he was wearing an open face type of helmet I left it on him and cleared his airway and made sure he was still breathing. I then turned my attention to the younger of the two who had collapsed. The moment I set eyes on him, I knew he was dead and despite my frantic efforts I could not revive him. It was with great sorrow that the young boy, who I now know to be Stephen Dodd, died. I received a "General Officer Commanding" commendation for my efforts that day, but nothing can make up for the fact that a young boy lost his life. Every time I think of that tragic day it still pains me.

We continued our boring routine at Rapier Barracks, Kirton, Lindsey. We carried out guard duties servicing vehicles over and over. There seemed to be no end to it, and I was beginning to get fed up, as were most of the lads. There was nothing to do and when there is nothing to do the army will invent things. We were given bullshit jobs for the sake of it. Our opportunity to escape from the perpetual boredom came on the day our Easter leave was due to begin. I was walking back over towards the compound when I met Mac.

"Scouse, guess what?" he said with a smirk on his face.

"Fuck off Mac!" I said suspecting he was about to start winding me up saying my leave was cancelled.

"No listen," he said, "we're all wanted over the compound because Argentina have invaded some islands belonging to Britain!"

"Oh, fuck off!" I said laughing, "you're one sad bastard if you think I'm going to believe that shit!"

"Okay, have it your way," he said, "but you will see when you reach the compound." I dismissed it from my mind totally as I continued back to the compound dreaming of my Easter leave.

As I neared the troop office I saw that everyone was fell in, but I put it down to the fact that it was it was a final parade before leave.

"Scouse, where the fuck have you been?" shouted one of the sergeants as I approached.

"The pay office," I lied.

"Well, get fell in!" he said. "Are there any more of 'G' troop over the block?"

"I haven't been over the block," I replied, thinking he was trying to catch me out.

"Stop fucking about, Scouse," he said with a very serious tone. "Is there anybody still in the block?"

"Well," I replied, "when I dropped my pay statement into my room, I didn't see anybody."

"What the fuck's going on?" I asked one of the lads as we waited outside the troop offices. He confirmed everything Mac had said.

An appearance by the battery commander told us all that this was no joke. "Right, listen in!" he shouted. "Argentina have invaded a group of Islands belonging to Great Britain, and as I speak a task force is being assembled to go and recover those islands, and we, 12 Air Defence Battery, will be joining them to provide air defence cover. Easter leave is cancelled!

"Where are these Islands?" someone shouted.

"Eight thousand miles away," was the reply.

"So getting there on a white bus is out of the question," he shot back.

Suddenly Kirton in Lindsey wasn't as sleepy anymore and my life was about to change forever.

4

The whole barracks became a hive of activity. Soldiers were running everywhere and within a matter of hours Rapier barracks had made a transition from being a boring, lifeless place to one of intense excitement. As we, 'T' Battery, were the only battery from the regiment going to the Falklands, we were able to borrow spares for the rapiers off our sister battery, who looked on in amazement and disappointment that they were not invited to the party. So stagnant had we become as a regiment, that now the call had come for some real action, we were not sure what to do. Thankfully the senior ranks came to their senses and quickly began to organise everyone.

To my utter disbelief, we were able to exchange any damaged or threadbare items of uniform. Normally, when going to the clothing store, run by a Staff Sergeant Seaman, he would just scowl and say 'fuck off'. I never once saw the man smile or say anything nice to anyone and his sole purpose in life seemed to be to give soldiers as hard a time as possible. His two equally useless side kicks would stand behind him shouting 'yeah, go on, fuck off!' Most of the lads loathed the three of them, useless as real soldiers, the reason they were in the stores in the first place. Much to Seaman's dismay, word had come from above to allow us any exchanges, no holding back. Seeing Seaman's face as all the lads descended on to his precious stores like a swarm of locusts was wonderful.

Unfortunately, Tony Wilson had left the army, so the crew for our Rapier, callsign 31D, would be Sergeant Stewart Burton (Commander) the very able Geordie Henwood, Paul Miller, Rob Green (Chimp) and me. We all worked non-stop for three days carrying out kit exchanges and being vaccinated, although what for we were never told. Most important, we carried out the testing and adjusting of the Rapier's Ts and AS. This involves running the system up to a high state of readiness. That way, any faults could be detected and sorted out. Nothing was left to chance with this. If it came to it, we needed to know the system would work.

During the brief respites in our work schedule, Mac and I would get together and discuss the possibilities of all the sabre-waving actually coming to a real fight. Mac was of the same opinion as me. It would all die down, either the Argentines would back down, having made their point, or more likely the British government would realise that the bluff had not worked and try for a solution through diplomatic channels. We both hoped, however, that it would come off. Anything was better than the boredom, even war!

The seriousness of the situation began to dawn on us with the arrival of the top brass. Such was our cosy little existence that we were hardly ever visited by anyone. On Saturday, 3rd April, we were honoured with a visit from the General Officer Commanding North East District. Major General Ian Baker, the same officer who had presented me with my commendation the year before for my efforts over the motorcycle crash. The general wished us luck and said that we were fine soldiers who were far superior than the enemy we would face. I think he meant it and I liked him for it

Finally, on Sunday, 4th April, after three hectic days of preparation, we set off for the sixteen hour journey to Plymouth. The soldiers on guard duty waved us off as we drove out of the gate in the white buses. Even some of the residents of Kirton in Lindsey had turned out to wave us off.

"Fuck me, Scouse, I can't believe we are doing this," Mac said to me.

"I know," I replied and I went on to tell him that I had rung my father to say that some troops had invaded a remote island belonging to Great Britain, but at the time I could not recall which islands or where the troops were from. I had told him that I was going but not to worry as it would most likely be called off anyway. Even by this time, though, I was not now nearly so sure.

On our arrival in Plymouth, we were given a police escort through the town. It seemed like half the locals were out to greet us.

"Give the spicks a good hiding!" they shouted. "Give em a smack from us!"

Some of the girls lifted their tops. "Get a look at these boys," they said, with their boobs hanging out. We turned in to Devonport Docks, which was closed off to the public. The ship we were going to embark on was the *Landing Ship Logistic (L.S.L.) Sir Geraint* which was already in dock. These ships are basically troop carriers and are manned by the Royal Fleet Auxiliary, though they also have many Chinese crew on board. The ships carry around 350 troops plus stores but I suspected we were to carry more. The next two days were spent on loading stores and all the other million and one things needed to fight a war on the other side of the world. As we were all unfamiliar with the task of loading a ship despite help, many mistakes were made and tempers became a little frayed, but eventually we finished.

On the evening of 6th April 1982, we set sail. There were no crowds of people on the dock to wave us off, only a few dockers who were quietly going about their work. They paid us no attention until one of the lads decided to throw his loose change down onto the dock. Very quickly half the ships contingent had joined in, much to the delight of the dockers below. They were running around scooping up all the cash as fast as they could. I stayed on deck with Mac until all had faded into the darkness. As soon as I made my way down below into the accommodation and saw the number of men squeezed into a confined space, I realised this was no pleasure cruise.

We quickly settled into the ship's routine, we had no option. With us on board were 29 Commando Regiment Royal Artillery who we would be attached to. They operate primarily in the frozen countryside of Norway, so their arctic warfare skills are first class. We were lucky because they passed on their expertise to us. These boys are the élite. They can deliver devastating firepower very accurately with their 105mm Light guns.

The Chinese members of the crew seemed to want to keep themselves to themselves, even to the point of rudeness, not even replying to a polite hello. I could only imagine that they had been on the receiving end of some army hospitality in the past.

Our senior officers very quickly dispelled all the rumours circulating that we would turn round at Ascension Island and return home having called the Argentine's bluff. We were left in no doubt that the training we would undergo on the journey should be taken seriously. As we passed the Bay of Biscay, I was sitting in the galley with Mac eating breakfast when a wave of nausea swept over me. I turned to Mac and he too was looking rather ill. The penny dropped, we were seasick. By the end of the day quite a few of the lads had taken to their bunks, much to the amusement of the Chinese crew. After a few days in our bunks recovering, we started training properly.

The training took in all the knowledge we would need to fight in very inclement weather conditions. Arctic warfare, first aid, all the weapons we would have when we landed, including hand grenades and antitank weapons. Our real objective though, was air defence and we began to learn something of the enemy we would face. By all accounts the Argentine Air Force was going to be a formidable enemy, and it was our task to shoot them out of the sky. At each intelligence briefing, the Argentine Air Force seemed to grow, and I suspected our officers were holding back, perhaps giving us the bad news slowly.

Life on board the ship was more than unpleasant because of the cramped conditions. There was no space not filled with soldiers' kit or soldiers bedded down. Living in these close confines and the pressure of our tight training schedule seemed to bring out the worst in people's characters. Some of the lads were bending over backwards to help each other, but there were the selfish ones who were only interested in looking after themselves. I had not taken much notice of these characters in the barracks, but now that I could see them for what they were, I quickly grew to despise them.

Fights would break out sporadically and sometimes for the most trivial reasons. The senior ranks were worried and the battery commander, Major Smith, ordered everyone into the galley for a lecture on the fine art of patience. The mood of the men, though, was revealed when halfway through his talk a fight broke out! The lads seemed to be determined to kick the shit out of each other. Mac and I spent most of our time up on the deck watching the other ships of the assembled task force. It was the only sanctuary from the claustrophobic madness that was life below decks.

As the weeks of intensive training passed, people began to tire of the cramped conditions and the food, or what was no excuse for food. We were served the same slop day in day out. The soldiers would shuffle along in the galley until they reached the hotplate where the Chinese crew would ladle it onto our metal trays. They would just chuck it on, so most of the time the clear tepid water they called soup would spill onto the pudding, which was always mandarins. Before long the lads were sick of the sight of bloody mandarins, but it was the only food they served and we had no choice but to eat it. So packed was the galley, I would try to find a place to stand and eat the slop as fast as I could.

On the rare occasions we were not involved in some form of training, we were obliged to help the Chinese crew with various chores around the ship. One day I was unlucky enough to be picked to help in the galley. It was a nightmare. Besides the unbearable heat and lack of space, the floor was covered in a layer of thick grease. I could hardly stay on my feet, and the constant movement of the ship made it even more difficult. I was put to work peeling potatoes over a huge sink with a Chinese crewman watching over me. He was not impressed with my efforts at spud bashing.

"No peel too thick!" he kept shouting. In my haste to show him I could do it I caught myself, the knife cutting my hand.

"Bastard!" I yelled out, cursing myself. Unfortunately, the Chinese crewman thought my abuse was aimed at him.

"You call me bastard, you call me bastard!" he kept repeating as he picked up a meat clever.

"No, not you," I pleaded, trying to calm him down as I backed away, but as the ship lurched I slid closer to him. I had visions of my father being informed of my death at the hands of a crazed Chinaman. Eventually, the other cooks managed to calm him down and as soon as I had finished my chores, I scarpered making a mental note not to cross him again.

Luck, though, was not on my side. A few days after my escapade in the galley, Mac and I were put on fatigues helping the Chinese cooks load potatoes from the deck to a store room below. It was back breaking work and as we had now moved into a hotter climate the sweat was pouring off us both. As with all fatigues, we had a cook watching over us in case we began to slack. If the cook spotted a bad potato he would yell 'bad one! bad one!' and so we would throw it overboard and the cook would turn back round leaning on the handrail enjoying a smoke whilst gazing out to sea.

'The lazy bastard!' I whispered to Mac carefully so I wouldn't be overheard.

As we were stooped down sorting the potatoes, Mac pointed above the cooks head. As I turned to look, a potato the size of a well-grown turnip flew past and hit the cook on the head with such force I thought he was going to fall overboard. I turned to look at Mac who by now was back to innocently sorting through the potatoes. I knew it was pointless trying to explain so I took to my feet and ran before the cook could recover. Such was my fear, I persuaded one of the lads to go and plead my innocence.

"What did he say?" I enquired on his return.

"He said he's going to cut your throat and throw you overboard!" was the reply. Every time I saw the cook after that, he made a cutting movement across his throat.

The arduous training regime we had undertaken since leaving Plymouth was now paying off. I certainly felt fitter than I had in a long time. We practised fire drills until we could do them in our sleep, but they lacked realism because we were all convinced that we would probably reach Ascension Island and be ordered home. We played the game because we had to. The intelligence reports on the Argentine Air Force continued to pour in but on more than one occasion they contradicted what the last report had said. I began to wonder if the officers were making some of it up or, at least, adding their own bits to it. The one thing we desperately needed was practice firing our rapier missile systems. This after all was the task we would have to carry out if we did reach the Falklands. But they can only be fired from land not a ship bobbing round at sea.

After what seemed like a life time we arrived at Ascension Island under the cover of darkness. There was nothing to see except the odd light twinkling in the distance. At first light Mac and I joined the other lads up on deck to get our first look at Ascension Island. Though it looked pleasant with its volcanic rock and nice beaches, it wasn't the island that caught my attention, but the amount of ships that surrounded us and the many helicopters that had taken to the sky with all kinds of military ordinance slung underneath them.

"Fuck me!' I said to Mac, 'I think we might really be going to war!"

"This is more than a show of strength," he replied. "I think Maggie means business." It was a shock to see so many ships as we had become so isolated in our own little world on board the *Sir Geraint* that we had forgotten this was a major military operation and we were a part of it. I had my first look at the *Canberra* and being a pleasure boat she looked perfectly at home, her bright white form reflecting of the blue waters of Ascension, but it belied her menacing cargo of Royal Marines and Paratroopers.

The stop at Ascension Island also presented us with the opportunity to reload our equipment. It was decided that in our haste to load up at Plymouth we had stacked priority ordinance IE, the Rapiers, behind less urgent equipment. I also decided that this would be a good time to write a final letter home to my family. Mac couldn't understand why I decided not to write any more letters. I felt that if we did continue south after our stop at Ascension we would surely be on a serious war footing and any news I was able to give my family would be very much out of date by the time they got it. They could even receive a letter saying I was fine when in fact I might be dead. It wasn't that I wanted to cut them off, I wanted to concentrate on what lay ahead. I look back at this decision now and it was undoubtedly selfish, but I was young and in all honesty scared at what would happen to me.

After a few days it was decided we would practise a beach landing and then hopefully fire off a few missiles to hone our skills and also carry out any further testing and adjusting (Ts & As) of the Rapiers. I couldn't understand the point in a beach landing because if we ever did get to the Falklands we would land by helicopter. Getting down the side of the ship and on to the landing craft was more difficult than I had imagined, more so fully loaded with kit. The landing craft would rise up on the tide, nearly wiping us off and then it would drop ten feet or so. We had to time the moment we jumped with great care. To hesitate could have resulted in serious injury. I made it, but only just. Our landing on the beach provided the Royal Marine spectators with the best laugh they had had in years.

Our landing was followed by a wait of several hours for the Rapiers to be flown off. The sun burned down on us as we sat there some of the lads peeled off their smocks as though they were on holiday. The cries of sunburn would be heard for days.

Later that day the Rapiers were finally flown off the ship and we were told that we could fire the following day. We would sleep on the island that night. The buzz went round that there were poisonous spiders on the island, so I tried zipping my sleeping bag up with a small hole to breath through but after five minutes I had to give up because of the heat.

The following morning we put the first of the Rapiers into action ready for firing and almost immediately word came through that we were to return to the ship. This was a blow. We were desperate to fire so that any problems could be sorted out, but it wasn't to be. Orders were orders and we returned to the ship, although there was a sense of excitement in the air that at last something might be about to happen. Our excitement, though, was short lived. Nothing happened and we stayed anchored off Ascension for nearly another week until, under the cover of darkness, we weighed anchor and slipped away. I knew now that there would be no turning back. Although I was prepared for what lay ahead, I realised that men were certainly going to die and I kept thinking that one of them could be me. What was war going to be like? Would I be brave? Would I be a coward? I just couldn't imagine myself in amongst it all. I giggled at my own naivety walking in the door of the local army careers office in Birkenhead. At that time my role in life was making chocolate biscuits and now I was on my way to war. As a young boy I had listened to the old men and their reminiscences and exploits of the second world war, but I never imagined them to be like the frightened young man I was now.

The mood on board *Sir Geraint* had changed and we all accepted that we were going to land on the Falklands. Only a last minute change of heart by the Argentinians could prevent war and, as we were told, this was highly unlikely. Within days of leaving Ascension Island the temperature dropped and we got our first feel of the cold South Atlantic winds. We had even taken to wearing our arctic clothing while up on deck, going through the endless weapons training. The briefing we were given on the weather conditions in the Falklands was somewhat vague. Some of the lads seemed to think we would be fighting in deep snow, others were of the opinion it was just wet and windy, and by all accounts the local population were a backward bunch of hillbillys. I decided I would keep an open mind and see it for myself.

The sinking of the Argentine ship the *General Belgrano* and the subsequent sinking of our own *H.M.S. Sheffield* left me in no doubt that the gloves were off. My reaction was that of most on board when the *Belgrano* was sunk. We laughed and said 'serves them right', but when we lost *H.M.S. Sheffield* we cried foul and called the Argies 'sly little bastards' and swore revenge when we landed. The real horror, pain, and suffering of the crew on those ships escaped us. We hadn't yet seen it for ourselves.

Two days out from the Falklands we began our final

preparations for the landing and were told the location of our Rapier sites would be Port San Carlos. San Carlos was chosen because it was covered by hills on both sides and was to some extent protected. Quite how protected would remain to be seen. We were issued with our small arms ammunition and I was also going to carry two rounds for the Carl Gustav 84mm anti-tank gun. We were also given morphine syretts for our own use only in the event of injury.

San Carlos was located around fifty miles from Port Stanley the capital, and it was known that there were some Argentians in the area. These were to be taken care of by the Paras and Marines and our main concern was the threat from the air. It was felt that we would almost certainly come under attack as soon as the Argies realised we had landed. Even at this late stage, I could hardly believe that we were going to fight. Surely somebody somewhere would step in and say enough is enough.

I had my last shower and rechecked my equipment for the hundredth time to make sure everything was where it should be. I could afford for nothing to come loose because there would be no second chances. We had made our wills out shortly after we had sailed, not that I had anything to leave. For the first time in months, though, my bank account was in the black. I went and sought Mac out, he was sitting on his bunk, deep in thought.

"You okay?" I asked him. "Yes," he replied "I've sorted my kit out. Have you done yours?"

"Yes," I nodded. "There's fuck all to do now but get on with it." We sat and chatted while we watched people filling magazines, cleaning their rifles and generally keeping themselves busy. For the first time since leaving Plymouth we were left alone to get on with what needed doing and when the army allows this, its a sure sign that something nasty is on the horizon.

It came over the ships tannoy that there was going to be a

church service in the galley for all those amongst us who wanted to make our peace with God. Mac turned to me,

"Scouse, you up for it?"

"Why?" I replied, "do you feel like getting your sins off your chest?"

"Well, sort of," he said, "this is as good a time as any." Though I was reluctant at first, the service gave me the chance to say my prayers and I felt better for it. Mac and I also made a promise to each other that if either of us were killed we would visit each other's family.

I suddenly felt exhausted so I went to my bunk, lay down and went into a deep sleep. The blaring noise dragged me back to the real world:

"RISE AND SHINE ITS TIME TO KILL THE ARGENTINE!" I looked over at Mac who was already up sorting through his kit. Seeing me awake he shouted over,

"This is it, Scouse. We're here."

"Can you actually see the Falklands?" I enquired.

"Well, it's still dark," he replied, "but the outline of the hills is visible. Come on let's go and see." I opened the door and the first thing I noticed was the smell. I could smell the grass and the scent of land. Already the helicopters were busy ferrying people and stores ashore. The Marines and Paras would go first and then our battery so we could set up our Rapiers to provide air defence cover before first light. After an eight thousand mile journey, the Royal Fleet Auxiliary had landed us to within a few feet of our objective. They had come up with the goods in this war, now it was our turn.

5

Men began to pull on their equipment. The tannoy ordered Air Defence crews to close up. All the members of 'T' Battery assembled together in the accommodation deck. All the various Rapier crews huddled together waiting for the order to proceed to the helicopter deck for the short flight to the shore. I had a good look around me to make sure I could see all the crew of our Rapier 31D. Stewart Burton was busy giving Geordie Henwood some last minute instructions for Chimp and Paul Miller. Looking around the sea of men smeared in camouflage cream it was hard to make out who was who in the dull light before I spotted Mac. He smiled and I gave him a weak grin back. Words were not needed. I prayed he would be okay. It was unlikely I would see him until after the war had finished.

We stood in position packed like sardines for what seemed like hours. The sweat was pouring down our faces. Men jostled each other to find a more comfortable position and take some of the weight off our backs. Some of the lads were cracking jokes to relieve the stress and the boredom and when word filtered down that it was daylight we began to panic. As air defence soldiers we were all fully aware that we were now very vulnerable to air attack. It was obvious that something had clearly gone wrong with the landing as we should have been ashore in darkness. Some the lads began to curse at what they considered to be the inept way the landing was being handled by the top brass. In reality it was nobody's fault; war is a complicated business and mistakes are made.

In the distance a ship's siren started up, followed immediately by most of the other ships in the bay. I wasn't sure what this indicated, but I knew that it meant danger. Then the tannoy warned us that it was 'AIR RAID RED.' We all surged forward.

"Stand still!" shouted an authoritative voice. Moments later we could hear the clatter of small arms fire, the distinctive thump of the Orlikan anti-aircraft guns that were mounted on some of the ships, and then the unmistakable sound of aircraft screaming over.

"Fuck, we are being attacked!" someone screamed. My throat suddenly went very dry. I could feel the fear in my stomach, I just wanted to get off the ship and on to land. I was scared, very scared, and when I looked into the eyes of comrades and friends I could see the same fear. I was certain that if I didn't get out soon I would throw up. I said a silent prayer.

"Please, God, if you look after me now I will be good. I will never do anything wrong again. I beg you for this chance, please."

"AIR DEFENCE CREWS TO THE HELICOPTER DECK" the tannoy barked.

"Right, let's get the fuck out of here!" Stewart Burton screamed, but it was impossible to squeeze past all the soldiers up the stairs to the helicopter deck.

When I eventually made it to the upper deck, I was greeted by the sight of soldiers lying all over the place trying to take cover. We moved aft towards the helicopter deck. The sun was shining brightly on the hills that surrounded us. So this was it, the Falklands! It was so different from what I had imagined it could have been the Outer Hebrides. I reached the helicopter deck with the rest of my crew to find Mac already there with his crew. A Sea King helicopter landed with a bump and Mac jumped on without a backward glance. The helicopter lifted off the deck, swung in low towards the shore and he was gone. There were helicopters flying in all directions as they ferried men ashore from all the ships in the bay. I was astounded to see the *Canberra* looking so white and large, just sitting there unloading her cargo of Marines and Paras. Surely the Argentine Fighters would go straight for her?

"We're on the next helicopter," Stewart shouted over the din. I was in a semi-crouching position, but the weight of the two Carl Gustav anti-tank rounds I was carrying kept me from lying down. Seeing my dilemma, Stewart leaned over and shouted in to my ear, "It won't be long now, Scouse." I gave him the thumbs up.

I felt a panic as the ships' sirens began wailing and the now familiar clatter of guns began firing some way off in the opening to the bay.

"Air raid red! Air raid red!" screamed a voice through the tannoy. Whoosh! An Argentine Mirage screamed down the bay hugging the contours of the land. It was followed by thousands of tracer, fired from the troops already deployed on the hills. A second later another jet screamed past. This was followed by a huge explosion.

Something had been hit, but I couldn't see what it was. The jets ducked and weaved, banked and turned and disappeared behind the hills. Then they were gone. Moments later, two more appeared and the clatter of machine gun fire built up into a crescendo as each individual soldier tried to bring the Argentine pilots crashing down. Panic set in as we waited for the helicopter and all respect for rank evaporated as soldiers fought for safer positions on the deck. Gunners were telling officers to 'fuck off' because they were trying to steal their safe havens. It all ended as quickly as it had begun, but now we had had a taste of what to expect and there wasn't a man among us who wasn't scared.

I saw the fear on the faces of the senior ranks in our battery, men I looked up to because they were the old sweats. They had years of experience under their belts, had patrolled the streets of Northern Ireland while I had been in school, but when it came to this they were no harder or different to me, they were in mortal fear for their lives. In this we were all equal. The smoke from the enemy bombs drifted across the bay as encouraging shouts that some of the jets had been hit came from below, but we had also taken casualties. One of our ships had been hit, but to my amazement the *Canberra* was left unscathed.

Everybody lay still for a moment, wondering what to do immediately after the air raid. Then the helicopters that had landed ashore for cover began to take off again. A Sea King helicopter swung in low and landed on our heli deck and we were beckoned forward by the load master. We ran forward and jumped on. I was second to last on board and so was nearer the door. It felt safer, but given the amount of kit I was carrying I would have sunk like a stone if we had gone down. We had barely lifted off the deck when the helicopter suddenly descended and we bumped on to the ground. We had landed. Each of us knew our job and we all set about our tasks without a word. Chimp and I began digging the trenches. Stewart and Geordie were preparing a site for the Rapier which would be arriving slung under a helicopter at any moment. Dusty Miller was busy preparing a place for the one ton Landrover D.S.V which held the radio and Rapier ancillaries on board.

Chimp and I were digging frantically. Normally on exercise digging trenches was a boring affair and we would take our time, but today we had some inspiration courtesy of the Argentine Air Force. The sweat was pouring off us despite the cold chill in the air. We had dug down no more than two feet when the trench began to fill with water, but we had no option but to carry on. Even at this early stage I realised that the low boots that were issued to the British forces at the time were useless. My feet were soaked.

Once more the ships' sirens began wailing to warn us of an imminent air raid.

"Oh Fuck, here we go again," Geordie shouted. As we were still waiting for our Rapier we were left with only our small arms to defend ourselves. Between us we had three rifles and two sub machine guns, the latter being low-velocity, and they were almost useless against fast flying aircraft. I could feel the fear rising in my stomach as I heard the ships in the bay firing at the advancing aircraft. Moments later, I spotted three Skyhawk jets streaking towards us. They looked oblivious to the rounds being fired at them from the troops and ships in the bay. I fired a full magazine of rounds at them, but it was useless and they were gone. Columns of smoke were rising someway off in the bay, but I could not tell what had been hit. The air raid over, we jumped out of our water filled trenches.

"Is everybody okay?" Stewart asked. Afterwards we were all talking non-stop about what we had just seen.

"Fuck me," Chimp said in his thick Geordie accent, "did ya see the bastards go, man?" One of the Skyhawks had gone over the hills trailing thick black smoke and Chimp said he had seen another spiralling towards the ground followed by a huge fireball. I hadn't seen it, but if it was true at least we were hitting back. The helicopters began to fly again and two Sea Kings flew in low across the bay one carrying our Rapier and the other carrying our one ton Landrover (D.S.V.). They were quickly joined by a third helicopter carrying a pallet of missiles. We were in business. Once they landed we swung in to action to get the Rapier operational ready for firing. After the various testing and adjusting (Ts & As), we loaded four missiles on to the beams. We were now ready to fire!

We used the empty missile crates and the spare earth from the trenches to fortify the rather vulnerable tracker. This was topped with turf and a camouflage net and even from a short distance it blended in well.

I now had a better chance to look at my surroundings. The Marines and the Paras were digging in on the hills like little ants. San Carlos settlement was only a stone's throw away. It was nothing more than a small collection of houses with brightly painted roofs of red and blue, but now there was a lot of military activity in the area. The ground was covered in a very coarse tussock grass, which was very difficult to walk over. The foot soldiers had my sympathy. Already our immediate area had turned into a quagmire, the only consolation being that the weather was good and not the gale force blizzards I had expected. This, though, was a double edged sword, because it left us at the mercy of the Argentine Air Force.

We had a radio and could now be given a more advanced warning of any air raids. It wasn't long before we heard the voice of Staff Sergeant Dixon at our Battery Headquarters (B.H.Q.).

"Hello, all stations. This is zero one zero, bogeys, (enemy fighters), your location, one zero minutes, out." Stewart ran and jumped into the operator's seat of the Rapier. Though this was not his job, he was eager to shoot a plane down himself. The wait for the attack in some ways seemed worse than being attacked, because during the raids we were kept busy trying to shoot them down.

The noise of gunfire at the opening to the bay grew once more in to a crescendo as every man and his dog fired at the attacking Skyhawks. It was impossible to keep track as they criss-crossed each other, trying to avoid the tracer rounds arching up towards them. The Skyhawks fired their cannons as they swept over the hills. The smell and smoke of cordite from the thousands of weapons being fired drifted across the bay. There was a huge bang and roar, as one of a missiles fired off the beams of the Rapier. Stewart had his target and I watched in an almost trance like state as the glowing missile hurled across the sky in pursuit of a fleeing Skyhawk. A man was fleeing for his life and we all stood there hoping for it to end in repayment for the destruction he had just wreaked upon us. It was not to be. The Skyhawk dropped behind a hill and the missile exploded. Now out of range he lived to fight another day.

"Fuck! Fuck!" Stewart cursed at his luck, "I nearly had the bastard." We each criticised Stewart for his performance saying we could have done better, but in reality we couldn't have. If the target goes out of sight the chase is up.

As darkness fell we continued to work on our position and we had a chance to eat our first food of the day. Not surprisingly, the field rations were far better than the food we had been served on the ship. We learned the tally for the day's events, though not by radio. It was not yet secure and the Argentinians would almost certainly be listening in. The *HMS Ardent* had been sunk and *HMS Antelope*, though still in the bay, had two one thousand pound bombs festering inside her. The Argentinians had lost sixteen aircraft which, if true, meant we had certainly given them a bloody nose. But at what price? I asked myself, and could we continue to take such losses with our ships?

I drew the 'Two AM till Four AM' stag, which didn't leave me with much chance of sleep. During the darkness I would feel the vibrations through the ground as the gunners of '29' Commando Regiment pounded the Argentine positions with their 105 light guns. The erupting flash would silhouette the gunners as they went about their macabre business. I also noticed how much colder it was after dark. I had managed to put on a dry pair of socks and like all the other lads I donned a pair of rubber chemical warfare boots which were awkward and clumsy but they compensated for our inadequate footwear. I sat there listening to the static of the radio in the blackness. It was an eerie feeling knowing that there were men all dug in around me, but I couldn't see or hear them, I could just make out the silhouettes of the ships in the bay especially the great white hulk of the *Canberra*. The poor bastards had taken a beating and this was only the beginning. I wondered what my family and friends were doing. Would they know we had landed yet? I woke Chimp for his stag and we talked for a while and we both confessed our fear at what daylight would bring. I crawled into my sleeping bag exhausted but sleep didn't come easy as my mind was replaying the air raids. It seemed like I had just fallen asleep when I felt a boot prodding me awake.

"Scouse, come on get up." It was Stewart Burton. "Come on," he urged, "stand to." In every army in the world soldiers will stand to at first and last light because this is the most likely time an enemy will launch an attack.

We switched the Rapier up, carried out the necessary testing and adjusting and waited for daylight and Round Two with the Argentine Air Force. They never came at all that day and it was a huge mistake on their part because it gave the task force time to establish a beachhead unhindered. I watched the endless amounts of ordinance coming ashore. The helicopters ferried troops from the ships all day long non-stop. We had one or two low risk 'air raid warning yellows', but nothing happened.

The lull in the battle, however, did not last. The Argentine Air Force returned just after first light the following day with a vengeance. The radio crackled in to life.

"Hello, all stations! 'Air raid warning red!' One five bogeys, I say again, one five bogeys! Your location, zero five minutes, out." I threw down the packet of dehydrated apple flakes I was eating for breakfast. My appetite disappeared. The now familiar racket of gunfire began someway off at the mouth of the bay.

At first I thought I had seen a flock of birds in the distance flying in all directions, frightened by the gun fire. Then I realised it was Argentine jets. They suddenly turned and headed up the bay so low that they passed below the masts of the ships anchored in the bay. The ships sirens began wailing belatedly as they were on us. One of our missiles left the beams with a bang. I tried to follow its path, but then more fighters came swooping over the top of us. I hadn't even seen where they had come from. I fired all my rounds at them and reloaded a fresh magazine in to my rifle as they flew across the bay dropping their bombs and firing their deadly cannons. We screamed in anger and terror at the jets as they banked and turned trying to find their targets. The pilots must have been shit scared seeing all the tracer arcing towards them. A Mirage fighter was screaming down the bay low and fast having just dropped its cargo of bombs when a missile shot up the back burner. The rear of the plane disintegrated into a huge fireball. It flipped over and nose dived into the water. I didn't see the pilot eject. One of our Rapiers called over the radio to confirm the kill as his. One pilot had managed to eject from his burning jet and was descending into the water. I couldn't believe he had not been hit by tracer as he floated down. I could see his white helmet bobbing around before a Royal Marine ridged raider boat was there to capture him. I was to learn later that this pilot had also been shot down by Rapier.

"Hello, all stations. This is zero one zero. Bogeys, your location, one zero minutes, out."

"Right, move your fucking arses!" Geordie shouted, "there are more of the bastards on the way! Let's get some missiles on the beams." The one missile that was still sitting on the beams had misfired and in normal peacetime conditions it would have been left for an extended period and then removed with great caution. Today we had no time for such niceties and the missile was dragged off and put to one side.

"Hello, all stations. This is zero C.A.P. Have intercepted. We now have four bogeys, your location, zero five minutes, out." This meant that the Harrier Jump Jets had caught the bastards on their way in to attack us and all credit to them because the Argies would have to run the gauntlet with them first. The smoke from the last raid hadn't cleared before the Argentine jets arrived. The leading jet disappeared over the hills trailing thick black smoke. It had been hit by some of the many thousands of rounds being fired at it. We fired a missile and it left the beams with a bang and a whoosh! I watched our missile as it gathered on line with a Mirage fighter, the pilot's white helmet turning to see the deadly glow of small arms fire from the hills and other Rapier missiles that had also been fired, all in pursuit of the same target. The Mirage exploded in to an enormous fireball. I wondered if the pilot had even tried to eject, but it was one less fighter to attack us.

The radio ordered us to a lower state of alert and we breathed a sigh of relief that for the moment we would be okay. After reloading the Rapier we huddled round the tracker drinking tea and giving our own opinions of what had happened. The truth was we were all shocked at the skill and bravery the Argentine pilots had shown and we were taking losses. As it grew dark we had our 'compo scoff' and filled our small flasks. They proved to be invaluable during the night while on stag because it was so cold. Geordie made one last brew before we got into our sleeping bags and left him to do the first stag. Geordie got to do first stag because he was the 2IC and so when he got to sleep it would not be interrupted, and Stewart being the commander would do last stag so he also got a nights sleep without any interruptions. Chimp and I being the last in the pecking order got to do the stag through the night.

I was about to take a sip out of my steaming mug of tea when the world turned white and I felt an immense heatwave sweep over me followed by a tremendous ear bursting bang. I found myself kneeling on the ground trying to make sense of what had just happened. Stewart and Geordie were shouting stand to but I couldn't see, my nightvision had gone. It felt as though I had had a camera flash fired directly into my eyes. Gradually, we learned what had happened. One of the bombs aboard *HMS Antelope* which was still anchored in the bay had exploded, ending the life of a brave man who was trying to defuse it and also badly injuring his equally brave assistant. Pictures of this incident were shown all over the world, but they showed the ship's magazine exploding and not the initial explosion.

For me personally this was a very low point in the war. The pent up fear, the air raids, the uncertainty of what each day would bring made me believe we would suffer many losses. Since my return from the Falklands people have often asked me what was it was like. There is really no answer for people who have not experienced it. In all fairness I have only ever received negative comments from idiots who prop up the bar of their local pub day in day out. The type who have the racing page hanging from their jeans pocket and have never ventured more than a bus ride from home. I have watched them solve the complicated issues of the world after they have just finished their tenth pint. They are sad people who think they are experts on every subject, but who are in fact ignorant fools.

We climbed into our sleeping bags feeling numb from both the cold and the events we had just witnessed. There was no way I could sleep. The explosion was playing over and over in my mind. Even the normally phlegmatic Geordie was left stunned. Paul, who was normally so quiet, voiced his concern but Chimp, true to form, was snoring away next to me. As we lay there in the freezing darkness of the tent, I whispered to Stewart who was now smoking more cigarettes than he normally did.

"Do you think there's any chance of us losing this war?" His cigarette glowed as he took a long drag from it.

"Why, Scouse?" he replied, "do you think we could lose?"

"Not really, but you never know."

"We could all get wasted, but then they will have Five Brigade to deal with."

"What fucking good will that be to us?"

'No good, but the name of the game here is to win, Scouse, and if that means you or I happen to die in the process, its hard shit. That's war."

While I was on stag I watched the ship burn fiercely and every few minutes some of the ammunition that was cooking in the heat would explode. Chimp stayed on stag with me for a while and we talked of all the things we would do on our return to England. It boosted our morale, but it also felt like it was a dream. This world we were now in was so far removed from normal life I could not even think that people back home were getting on with their everyday lives. It never occurred to me that all this would effect me in any long term way.

All the next day we watched the wrecked hulk of the *HMS Antelope* smouldering on the water. Eventually she broke her back and sank to the bottom of the icy waters of San Carlos Bay. The Argentine Air Force continued to press home their attacks with suicidal aggression, but as the weather was already moving in to a 'Falklands' winter the driving rain and wind began to hamper their efforts. Once again, however, it was a double edged sword. Living conditions became appalling. On one wet windy day Stewart called me over.

"Scouse," he said pointing to empty jerrycans, "go and get some water from the settlement."

"By myself?" I protested.

"Who the fuck do you want to take?" he answered.

"Well, can't Chimp give me a hand?"

"Oh, okay," he relented, "take Chimp with you, but any

fucking about and I'll fill you both in." As the most junior soldiers on our Rapier all the shit work fell on our shoulders, but as I had joined just before Chimp I made him lug the empty jerrycans.

Chimp, like me, was only too happy to be getting away from the Rapier for a while.

"If there's an air raid get your arses back here fast!" Stewart shouted after us. We followed a muddy track to the settlement crossing a small bridge were there were a few ducks playing.

"I will have one of those little bastards on the way back," Chimp smirked.

"How?" I asked. "If you go firing your weapon now Stewart or Geordie will kick your arse all over the place."

"Who said anything about shooting them?" Chimp said laughing. When we reached the settlement we decided to have look around in the hope that we could have something away. Our battery HQ was set up by some of the houses in the settlement, so we wandered over to their tents. I could not believe my eyes. They had the best of everything. There were huge tents complete with heaters and even a mess tent where the cooks were busy preparing hot food. This was certainly a different war to the one we were involved in. This was another world. Though Battery HQ had some of the more essential soldiers in its ranks, it also had some of the most useless tossers and Staff Sergeant Seaman and his two cronies fell comfortably in to this catagory. As we approached the tents he appeared quickly followed by his side kicks.

"What do you two twats want?" he yelled out.

"We've just come to get some water, Staff," I answered him.

"Well, get the fucking water and fuck off," he said, "and don't come back." His cronies burst out laughing and Seaman looked round enjoying every minute of it. I looked into his eyes with a hatred that I have rarely ever felt for another man and nothing would have give me more pleasure than to have lifted the rifle I was carrying and emptied every round in to this sad little bastard in front of me. Seaman looked at me for one moment and he caught the real hatred I felt for him.

"Come on, Chimp," I said loud enough for him to hear, "they're just shite." Seaman said nothing. He was nothing without his rank and he knew it.

We filled our jerrycans and made our way back to the Rapier. On the way I spotted a recently dug grave. The grave was of a Royal Engineer sapper and I was told by a lad standing near that he had died during an air raid. Whether it was true or not I never found out, but what was real was the fact that some poor sod had lost his life. I wondered if his family knew of the fate of their loved one. His grave was covered over by rocks and it brought home to me even more so than the sinking of *HMS Antelope* how crude all this was. Both Chimp and I said a prayer and carried on our way.

We reached the bridge and the ducks and Chimp told me of his master plan. To catch one he was going to throw his bayonet at them!

"Oh, fucking sure you are Chimp," I jeered, "and who the fuck are you, Audey Murphy?" Chip put his jerrycan down, pulled his bayonet from its scabbard and went into a half crouching position and moved towards the ducks. He threw his bayonet at the nearest duck hitting it on the head with the handle. The stunned duck sat there and Chimp picked it up and put it down the front of his smock. I stood there with my mouth open, gasping.

"Chimp, that was a fucking fluke," I said "you hit it with the handle!"

"I know," he replied, "I meant to, I don't like cruelty." Chimp handed the startled bird over to Stewart, who promptly gave him a smack round the ear and let it go again.

Though the air raids were now becoming more sporadic

and the Marines and Paras had started the push out towards
Port Stanley, the weather was certainly causing us some
problems. Everything was covered in mud or was wet and
damp, and as a result we were becoming more miserable.
Even so Stewart and Geordie would not stand for any
slacking. It was a losing battle. The news that we had lost the
Atlantic Conveyor, and the vital spares she was carrying early
on in the war had dropped our morale. I was listening into
the net one morning when an order came through detailing
a move to Bluff Cove for one of our Rapiers. I found this
odd because that particular callsign had radioed in saying
they had a fault and so could not fire. Stewart had also picked
up on this and he radioed HQ to volunteer our callsign as
we were fully operational, but his request was denied. Much
has been written on the mistakes of Bluff Cove, but having
spoken to a member of the Rapier crew who was sent there
while not operational, he feels that they could have made a
difference and possibly shot down the jet that bombed the
Sir Galahad. We shall never know but I feel that it was a
reckless decision to send a rapier to protect people when it
was clearly not operational.

6

I woke up one night with the most unbearable pain in my
ear. The pain was such that I could not get back to sleep. As
the day wore on the pain worsened and I began to feel sick
but in view of the situation we were in I mistakenly decided
to keep it to myself. I felt that the first aid station in the
settlement had enough to deal with and I didn't want to turn
up with an inflamed ear. Shortly after we had carried out our
normal Ts and As, I was standing by the tracker when my
head began to spin and in a moment I had collapsed. The
next thing I remembered was waking up in what looked like
an old potting shed with a Royal Navy doctor giving me an
injection into my arm.

"Aah, you're back with us," he said. I explained the pain
I had in my ear and after a examination he confirmed that it
was infected. After giving me some tablets, he said I would
feel better and the pain would ease off. I spent two days lying
on some old cot covered in sacking before the doctor would
be persuaded that I felt okay. I wandered back up to
our Rapier to be greeted by calls of "its your stag" and
"malingerer". I felt overjoyed to be back with the lads. I
realised after being away how just how filthy we all looked.
We had been together so long we didn't see it anymore. A
party of Royal Navy lads arrived one afternoon to bring us
some fresh bread, an act we were most grateful for. As they

came into the tent the smell of soap and aftershave was overwhelming. They smelt clean but what they smelled from us was obviously hard to disguise as they backed out of the tent bidding their polite goodbyes.

The days were now taken up by hours of boredom with the odd air raid and endless false alarms. We would be taken up to 'air raid yellow' and then 'air raid red' and then back down to 'yellow'. Our main preoccupation was to gather round the radio after stand to at last light. We would be given a 'sitrep' (situation report) and put requests for cigarettes or anything else we needed – within reason. Stewart and Chimp were going through vast amounts of the 'dreaded weed'. mostly out of boredom, but it would all bededucted from their pay after the war. It was during these sitreps that we learned of the battles won by the Paras, Marines and Scots Guards and it boosted morale. For a more detailed report we would tune in to the BBC World Service, broadcast eight thousand miles away, to find out what was going on our doorstep. During these quiet moments I would go somewhere private and read the letters still being sent by my family, but it was hard to take in. They spoke of everyday things back home, such as my dad's garden looking nice and Mrs Jones, who lived down the road, 'said to say hello'. I knew I had taken the correct decision to stop writing once we had passed Ascension. How could I possibly describe what I had been through? Even if I had written back saying it was all sweetness and light, they would have known it was rubbish.

As much as I respected the lads in our crew, we began to really irritate one another. It was only to be expected after what we had been through, but we began to get on each other's nerves. I had a punch up with Paul because he would continually taste the food as he cooked it and I accused him of eating more than his share. But my real gripe was that he would put the spoon back in to the pot from his mouth. He accused me of winding the watch forward when I was on stag so I could finish early. We couldn't have a go at Stewart, because he was as hard as nails, so we resorted to talking behind his back, calling him a complete tosser.

Our internal feuding, though, was halted one morning when the radio warned us of an imminent visit from the commanding officer (CO). This was viewed to be worse than an air raid. In a flurry of activity we tried to make the place and ourselves more presentable. A helicopter landed and the colonel sauntered over with his nose in the air, looking immaculate in his freshly ironed uniform. Stewart brought us to attention and saluted the Colonel.

"Stand at ease," he said with a wave of his hand. He then walked over to me. "What's it been like, er . . . Gunner, Gunner . . . er?"

"Gunner Denmark," I replied. "It was quite scary at first, Sir."

"Yes, quite," he said and moved on to Chimp. "How long have you been with us, young man?" he asked. Chimp's reply in his thick Geordie accent was completely lost on the colonel and he looked at Chimp puzzled. Wisely, he decided not to try and decipher what he had said.

"Would you like a cup of tea?" Stewart offered in an attempt to draw him away from Chimp. He looked at our catering arrangements and declined the offer. We all stood there waiting to hear the colonel give us a 'well done, boys, I am proud of you' speech but it wasn't to be. Instead he told us that one of our sister batterys was on firing camp in the Outer Hebrides and that they were bravely firing without the protection of hardened shelters. We all stared at each other waiting for the punch line. Surely it was a joke. What did he imagine we had been doing here? The colonel smoothed his trousers out.

"I must dash," he said. With that he walked over to his helicopter and was gone.

This was in complete contrast to a visit we received from

Major General Jeremy Moore who came walking up to our
site complete with his Bergen on his back. He sat and had a
mug of tea with us and asked if we had any concerns. He was
genuine and I liked the man. I knew that our fate could not
be in better hands.

Stewart decided to take a stroll down to the water's edge
one day and asked me if I wanted to tag along, more because
if he found any goodies I could carry them back for him. On
reaching the pebbled shore we were shocked at the amount
of debris that had been washed up from the *Antelope*. There
was everything from sailors' hats to television sets. It was
heart breaking to see all the men's personal effects, such as
letters and diaries, lying burned and scorched on the pebbles.
I picked one of the sailors' hats up with its band reading *HMS
Antelope*. Stewart, who I thought couldn't care less about
anything, looked rather gutted.

"Come on," he said, "it's not right to be looking at all their
belongings." We headed back, but that little trip taught me
that no matter how hard the exterior, there could always be
a softer person underneath.

Chimp and I were returning from a trip for water and
another barrage of insults from Seaman and his side-kicks,
when we passed a group of Royal Engineers who were
obviously excited about something. I heard one of them
mention Port Stanley.

"What's going on, mate?" I shouted over to one of them.

"Haven't you heard?" he replied. "The spicks have give
up! There's a white flag flying over Port Stanley!" Chimp and
I made our way back to the Rapier as fast as we could.

"Stewart! Have you heard?" I shouted.

"Yes, it's just come over the radio," he replied, "but don't
get too excited. We might still be here for a while yet." He
was right, but we were just so happy that it was over.

The days following the surrender were by far the longest.
There didn't seem any point in us being there, but the ever

cautious Geordie kept reminding us that it could easily kick off again.

'I don't trust the Spicks', he would say. That wasn't what we wanted to hear as our thoughts were now all about going home. Finally, the news we had been waiting for came over the radio we were going to be relieved by 9 Plassey Battery, one of our sister batterys who had arrived from the UK and, unfortunately for them, had missed all the action. Sadly, on their return, some of them told anybody who would listen that they had also been involved in the fighting, and to my utter disgust some of them even lowered themselves to showing pictures of dead Argentine soldiers around to back up their claims. Though all the members of this battery were awarded South Atlantic medals because they met the criteria by being within a certain distance from the Falklands, only a handful who were on attachment to T battery could say honestly that they had seen action. The morning of our departure arrived and we were packed and ready hours before first light like children waiting for Father Christmas. The Rapier and its ancillaries were staying with the new crew. We heard the characteristic whopping noise made by a Chinook helicopter and sure enough it was our relief crew. The huge beast landed and they came strolling down the rear ramp all fresh and clean and wearing every piece of arctic clothing they had been issued. They looked a bit shocked at our filthy appearance. We gave them a few war stories and in all fairness they were eager to know what it had been like. Walking up the ramp into that warm helicopter was wonderful, we all had huge grins on our faces. We made ourselves comfortable, it lifted into the air and we were off. Looking out of the window the scene below was one of tranquillity. The bomb craters were now full of water and the ducks were enjoying a swim in them. 'Nature repairing the damage caused by man', I thought. As the machine glided effortlessly over the difficult boggy ground I came to appreciate the epic march our soldiers had accomplished. I felt a warmth that I hadn't experienced in months, and I fell asleep.

The changing pitch of the helicopter's rotors as we descended woke me. I looked out of the window to get my first look at Port Stanley and the devastation was complete. There were buildings burnt down. Some of them were still burning. Military vehicles of every description lay abandoned. There were rifles, helmets, hand grenades and rounds of all kinds of ammunition strewn all over the place. We trudged through the mud and human shit to our temporary accommodation which was a laboratory that had been wrecked by the Argies. Worst of all, their excrement was wiped all over the walls. The equipment had been smashed up beyond repair. Any respect I had had for the Argies vanished there and then. We began to clean the place up and I felt like throwing up. I was overjoyed when Mac turned up.

"Scouse, where the fuck have you been? We've been here for ages. Its fucking great. We're going to have a good laugh." After swapping war stories, we set off to have a good look around. After hearing about Port Stanley non-stop for the last few months it was hard to believe I was here.

"These bastards will blow your tits off," Mac said, handing me a brand new Argentine FN rifle which was similar to our own weapon except that the FN had a full automatic capability. We fired off a few magazines and then threw the rifles away in search of more deadly toys like hand grenades. An Argentine jeep flew past, driven by some of our lads screaming and laughing like lunatics. One lad was chasing a chicken down the road firing a machine gun at it. It was utter chaos, with no law and order. Somewhere along our travels we managed to get hold of a bottle of vodka and began to get very very drunk. We staggered along laughing one minute and crying the next. We fired indiscriminately at vehicles and anything else we came across. Through a drunken haze we came across some French panard armoured cars and tried to drive them around, but it was hopeless. We even considered trying to fire the guns but once again we were too drunk to work them out. In amongst all this madness the residents of Port Stanley were trying to put their lives back to normal. We gave no thought to the horrors they had been through themselves. Their once peaceful community had been shattered and for people who were so private, they would have to live under the spotlight of the world's media. Though it didn't cross my mind at the time these people would never be able to have the life they lived before the invasion. That was gone for good.

"Come and look at this," one of the lads shouted. Mac and I staggered over to find the torso of a dead Argentine soldier still wearing some kind of military shirt. I looked at it but felt nothing. It didn't sicken me, it didn't make me sad.

I felt nothing. Moments later someone shouted 'GRENADE'! and we scattered. It exploded with a boom and after picking ourselves up we returned to find nothing left of the torso. The lad who threw the grenade was standing laughing hysterically. "That moved you, you bunch of knobs!" he screamed.

At some point in the night, Mac and I made our way back to the laboratory. The sound of gunfire could still be heard and judging by the empty sleeping bags some of our lads were still in the thick of it. There was also one or two who had black eyes and swollen lips; a few old scores had been settled. What happened next could very easily have ended in tragedy. One of the lads was ranting and raving how he was going to kill another member of the troop he had been arguing with. Mac and I had just passed this lad who was taking a piss outside. I thought it best to say nothing and let them sort it out in the morning, but then I heard the unmistakable sound of a rifle being cocked and Mac stepped forward and handed the lad the rifle.

"Go on big mouth," he said, "go and fucking do him then.

You are all fucking mouth, because he is outside having a piss." The lad snatched the rifle from Mac, his anger fuelled by alcohol, and ran outside. I then made one of the more stupid decisions of my life and went after him in the hope I could talk him out of it. When I got outside the lad was standing there. His quarry had fled, or more likely he had wandered off not realising that there was a drunken soldier armed with an automatic weapon after his blood. The rain was now coming down in sheets and we were both soaked to the skin.

"Come on," I said, "it's not worth it."

"Fuck off," he slurred "or I will fucking waste you." Here was a drunk with his finger on the trigger and the business end was pointing in my direction.

"Okay, it's up to you," I said, "but don't say I didn't try to stop you." I left him to it.

The following morning we were paraded and told that the events of the previous day were over. They had let us burn off some aggression but the party was over. We were told that we would be boarding a requisitioned ferry the *St. Edmund* to guard Argentine prisoners. This was good news because it meant we would be living in luxury in comparison to the laboratory. We would be able to get showers and wash our filthy clothes. More important, we would have toilets because quite a large number of the lads had gone down with acute diarrhoea and vomiting, Mac included. It wasn't surprising after having to clean up and live amongst human shit. We boarded the *St. Edmund* two days later.

On our approach to the ship from the jetty we could make out the faces of the Argie soldiers peeping through the portholes at their new guards. Some of the lads were making fists at them and they would disappear out of sight. After boarding we were shown to our cabins. I threw my dirty clothes into the washing machine and made my way to the showers. Some of the lads were already on their way back though I hardly recognised them looking as clean as new born babies. I stayed in the shower for ages, washing the months of dirt and grime away. The feeling of the hot water was out of this world.

That afternoon we were all gathered in the ship's restaurant to find out the guard rosters. The Argentine prisoners were divided up. The officers were put in to cabins similar to our own and the lowly conscripts were accommodated down in the ship's hold. They had all been given medical treatment where needed and some of them certainly needed it. They had festering wounds and sores, not through combat but because of the conditions they had had to live in. One of the conscripts had apparently taken his boots off and left a huge chunk of his heel still inside. Halfway through the briefing, I felt a bit light-headed and the onset of stomach cramps. For the next two days I was either on the toilet, throwing up or both.

I did my first prisoner guard with Mac, who took great pleasure in tormenting them and taking the piss out of them. This was my first real chance to see them up close and they were not children as has been suggested. In fact their age group matched that of our own Army, though they were certainly not what I would describe as professional soldiers. They were sloppy and lazy and didn't care much how they looked. The showers were now available for them to use, but if it hadn't been for our lads forcing them to use them they would have happily stayed filthy. Even when we took them for breakfast, they kept putting salt on their cornflakes instead of sugar, no matter how much we explained. I spoke to some of them and listened to their harrowing accounts of what they had endured since they had landed on the Falklands. They had no idea where they were or where the Falklands were situated and very few of them had expected it to be cold and desolate. One soldier told me that they had been warned that the British did not take prisoners and even that the British sometimes liked to eat them. I was amazed that they really thought that they would be eaten. By the Paras maybe but not us!

We guarded the prisoners carrying loaded weapons but I knew these people would never try anything. Why would they want to? After all, they were now living in luxury, getting medical and dental treatment, something they would not get even on their return home. The officers were very aloof at first, until we made it clear that they had lost through poor leadership. One particular officer even had the nerve to try and lecture me on how professional his soldiers were.

"If your soldiers are so professional," I answered, "why did they wreck so many buildings and shit all over them and wipe it up the walls".

"They never," he countered, "it's lies by your government."

"It's not lies," I replied, "because I was cleaning it myself." His face reddened and he stormed off.

If there was any work to be done on the ship we would pick volunteers from the conscripts as the officers were not allowed to work under some rule regarding prisoners of war. It would seem officers are the same the world over. I was escorting a group of prisoners when one of the lads with us approached me.

"Scouse, do ya want a laugh?"

"Why?" I replied with caution.

"It's all right," he said, "I won't hurt the prisoners."

"Well, what then?" I said. He put the group to work mopping up and then called one of them over. The Argie looked terrified. He obviously thought he was about to be beaten up or worse. We made our way along the corridor to where our own troops were sleeping and stopped outside one of the cabins. A lad from our troop was in there sleeping. The lad with me then unclipped his magazine and then emptied it and put it back on his weapon and handed it to the scared Argie. He then whispered to the Argie hands up and pointed towards the cabin. After some confusion the penny dropped and the Argie understood what we wanted. After opening the door, he walked in and said "ands upa." The scream from inside the cabin told us the joke had worked. The Argie then came flying out and handed the weapon back and hid behind us.

On the whole the prisoners were treated well and I think had the roles had been reversed we would not have been treated quite so well. That said, the French Red Cross were on hand to ensure there was no real maltreatment of the prisoners. They were all eventually taken back home to Argentina and we embarked on to the *M V Norland*, yet another requisitioned ferry. Again we lived in relative comfort and now there was alcohol on hand so we were able to get drunk, money permitting. But the lads were starting to get frustrated because most of the other units had left for home and we had been told nothing. I had managed to send a cable home telling my family that I was safe and well and thanking them for their support. Also on board with us were the Scots Guards who had fought so bravely on Mount Tumbledown. Like us the guards were eager to get home but they lost no time in re- adjusting their alcohol intake at the bar each night. They would consume vast amounts of beer while singing about past battles their regiment had won.

At last, orders came through that we would be sailing the following day for Ascension Island and then flying home via a refuelling stop in Dakar, West Africa. I stood on the outer deck as we sailed past the last piece of land that was jutting out. The sky was grey with a threat of snow and the cold icy south Atlantic wind was blowing in my face. Looking at the cold barren land I wondered why two civilised nations had gone to war over it. What was it about these islands the people had to die for? Any thoughts of us being the victors and the Argentines being the vanquished quickly evaporated, as I reflected on the loss of life and injuries suffered by both sides. Was the Falklands worth it? Well, I suppose for the people who came back to all the celebrations and the rather over-used shouts of hero, yes. For the senior officers who were given the promotion as a thank you, it certainly was, but for the families who had lost loved ones, the price was too high.

The week long voyage to Ascension passed in a succession of days getting drunk and sleeping. I had never slept so much in all my life. Mac and I would sit and talk for many hours about every subject except the Falklands, and on reflection it may have done us some good if we had talked about the war. Mac did admit that he felt like he had a black cloud hanging over him and I understood him because I also felt the same. I wasn't sure why because we should have been happy. I also felt anxious about our arrival in England. I was looking forward to seeing my family, but then, I didn't want to leave my mates after what we had been through together.

We reached Ascension Island and boarded a Royal Air Force jet for home. The journey was long and boring. The monotony was only broken by our brief stop in Africa. One hour out from RAF Waddington in Lincolnshire we were warned that there would be a lot of press waiting with our families. This came as a great shock, because I had planned to arrive home unannounced and go for a few drinks with my dad. As our plane touched down I caught sight of the crowds of people waiting. I could hear my sisters screaming in the crowd as I came down the steps of the aircraft with my mates. The Royal Air Force police tried in vain to hold them back but along with my sisters the crowd broke through.

The following night I returned home for a party with my family and friends and they asked, as I knew they would, what it was like. And though I tried desperately hard to tell them, I knew it was a waste of time. They had no understanding of what I had been through. I was telling one of my friends about how scared I had been in the air raids when he interrupted me and asked if I had seen any penguins. I had made it back home, but I was a different person to the one who had left all those months before. My experiences had changed me forever.

7

During my journey to the Falklands, like most of the single lads (and the odd married one!), I sorted out a few letters from the sack loads we had received from the lonely young girls back home. I made sure the few I wrote to were not too far from my home town. Then, should anything develop, I would not have to travel too far. I had received one reply I was interested in but once we had landed I had stuffed the letter in my pocket and had forgotten about it. Now I had a month's leave decided to follow it up. So I wrote once more to a girl called Sarah Leeson from Ainsdale, a little town near Southport, Merseyside, enclosing my phone number. A few days later the phone rang.

"Hi, could I speak to Edward, please?" asked the rather jolly hockey-sticks voice on the other end.

"Speaking," I replied.

"Hi, it's Sarah," she said. I was caught off guard at first and after mumbling a few words we began to chat. We got on great: In fact we were talking for over two hours. We made a date for the following night and I persuaded my sister to drive me to Southport. We had a wonderful night. I felt like I had known her all my life. At seventeen, Sarah was four years younger than me. She was still studying, hoping to become a nurse. Her mother worked in a local shop and her father was a housemaster at a private school in the south

NOT FOR QUEEN AND COUNTRY

of England. Sarah herself had attended a Swiss finishing school, made possible because her father had been teaching there at the time. I got to know her family quite well, but I always felt awkward in their presence. I now know it was because we had little or nothing in common. The conversation was always small talk about the weather, but sometimes her mother would dig for more information and what my chances were of promotion, what my family's occupations were and so on. I wasn't very forthcoming with any information, not because I didn't want to, I was just shy. I explained that I wasn't interested in promotion, I was happy as I was, but I could tell she was disappointed in me.

Despite our very different backgrounds we were soon dating and she began to occupy all my spare time when I was on leave. Back at the regiment things were far from good. It all felt rather pointless. My attitude was that we had been to war and the chances of going again were slim at best. This view was also shared by the majority of the lads, many of whom decided to leave. They had had enough. Whether I was influenced by the mass exodus I don't know, but one day I decided I had had enough, so I signed off. This effectively meant that I would be free to leave in one year's time. Mac was standing behind me when I signed off.

"Me too," he grinned. This meant we would be leaving around the same time.

We had just finished first parade when our troop commander Lieutenant Andrews called me over. I walked over to him and saluted smartly.

"You wanted to speak to me, sir?"

"Er, yes, Denmark," he replied. "There is a victory parade in London in two weeks time to honour the task force. It will end with a dinner in the Guildhall which will be attended by the Prime Minister Margaret Thatcher. You have been chosen to go."

74

"Well, thanks, sir," I beamed. I rushed over to tell Mac the good news.

"I know," he replied, "I am going, too." Mac grinned. "It will be a laugh."

"By the front quick march." We set off through the streets of London. Only a few men from each regiment had been chosen to attend so I was lucky. I felt so proud with my one and only medal pinned to my chest. The throngs of people each side of the street were tremendous. They were all shouting and waving. All the old boys were there with their rows of medals pinned to their chests. They were no doubt thinking back to their own past battles during the Second World War. One old soldier caught my eye as I was looking at his medals. I smiled at him and he gave me a weak grin. I was so proud to be British. The people were waving their Union Jacks for us, the conquering army returning to a heroes' welcome.

After the parade we had a wonderful meal in the Guildhall. I was seated with members of the of the Falkland Islands Police Force and the very brave Warrant Officer (WO2) Phillips. WO2 Phillips was assisting in the defusing of a bomb on *HMS Antelope* when it exploded. Although he had lost his arm, he had not lost his sense of humour. At his suggestion we all signed each others menus. Mine is displayed to this day on the former Falklands warship *HMS Plymouth* which is berthed as a tourist attraction in my home town of Birkenhead.

I looked over to see Mac who was seated across the hall with the Royal Marines. They were all laughing and being loud, swigging wine from the bottle. Mac was in good company. We all toasted each other and remembered those who would never return. T Battery 12th Air Defence Regiment was responsible for the downing of fourteen Argentine Aircraft. This figure was probably much higher as many

Aircraft were seen trailing smoke and therefore never made it back.

The parade over, we returned to the monotony of the regiment. The parade had lifted our morale. A pat on the back for our achievements. But now all we seemed to do was clean vehicles and sweep up, or worse, guard duty. Most nights we would be in the pubs getting drunk. Discipline had most certainly slipped because even the senior ranks had lost their enthusiasm. I was counting the days to my discharge. I gave no thought to what I would do when the time arrived and I had no job to go to. Such trivialities hadn't entered my head.

Every weekend I would go home. If I was unfortunate enough to have been put on duty I would pay someone to do it for me. I would also bribe one of my sisters for the use of her flat. They were special times. In fact, they were the only times me and Sarah had any privacy. On one such weekend I asked Sarah to marry me. I hadn't planned it. It just seemed the right thing to do. To my utter surprise Sarah accepted. Only on the train journey back to barracks did it sink in what I had committed myself to.

The following weekend I was summoned to Sarah's parents house. She had broken the news that we were planning to marry. I hadn't known what to expect when I arrived at the house but thank God her father hadn't been able to make it home that weekend. So it was only her mother to give me a roasting. Sarah ushered me up to her room. I had just sat down on the bed when her mother entered the room.

"Hello, Edward," she said in her soft Scottish accent. Pulling a chair up to the bed she sat down. Here we go I thought lecture time. I felt like a child in front of the teacher about to be scolded for not bringing homework in. "Sarah has told me and her father of your plans to marry," she said, staring me in the eye. For a moment I considered replying that I didn't know what she was on about and Sarah must be making it up.

"Well, er . . . yes, er . . . yes, we have," I replied in a whisper. My throat was suddenly very dry. She began a torrent of questions: Where will you live? What will you do for money, etc? I didn't have the answers she was looking for.

"We only want what is best for you," she relented. All we ask is that you don't rush in to things." I felt like telling her that there was little or no chance of that as I hadn't the money to buy her daughter an engagement ring, let alone run off and get married. I always had the feeling Sarah's mum was tolerating me rather like a spot that needs squeezing but if left alone it will go eventually away.

Mac greeted the news of my impending marriage with a grin and words to the effect of 'dickhead.' "Well, if it comes off," I replied, doubting it myself now.

Me and Mac spent all our spare time getting pissed and getting into mischief. One afternoon we were returning from a drinking session in Scunthorpe. I was walking ahead of Mac or rather staggering because we were well and truly pissed. We were on our way down a deserted country road when I spotted an old bike in a ditch. It had no tyres but I decided to ride it anyway. Looking behind me to gloat at Mac about my newly acquired transport I caught sight of him running towards me with a very flattened and bloody rabbit we had passed some way back down the road. Someone was going to get this over their head and it didn't take much brains to deduce that I was to be the recipient. I was in a quandary: should I ditch the bike and run for it? I decided to peddle as fast as I could. There was sparks coming off the metal wheels as they failed to grip the road. It was like a nightmare where you are being chased but getting nowhere. Just as Mac was about to transform the rabbit into a Davy Crockett hat for me, a car screeched to a halt.

"Ha! Ha!" I cheered at Mac, "saved!" Then I looked over to the car. In it was the second in command of the regiment. We were given a severe dressing down and ordered into the car. The journey back was in silence except for the odd 'idiots' hissed by the officer.

One night in a state of inebriation Mac and me thought it would be great fun to streak across the drill square. We set off wearing our boots and a bowler hat each. Where the hats came from I don't know. We moved across the square and stopped in some hedges opposite the guardroom. It was all I could do to stop laughing. We jumped from behind the hedge. The sentry stood staring at us not believing what his eyes were seeing.

"Fuck!" he mouthed and then finding his voice, "guard stand to," he screamed. We were all ready making good our escape. Looking over at Mac as we ran in his bowler hat and boots and his tackle swinging in the wind was a sight I shall never forget. We made it back to the accommodation block flew in to our room and locked the door.

I peeped through the curtains. There were soldiers moving through the barracks with flash lights. Then came a hammering on the door

"Open this fucking door now!" demanded a voice on the other side. I looked at Mac he shook his head. We stood firm. The handle began moving up and down followed by more hammering. Then we heard muffled voices.

"Sarge, they were seen going into another block," we heard a soldier say. The footsteps receded.

"That was fucking close," Mac said. There was some gossip about the incident the following day. Everyone had their own theories as to who the culprits were, except me and Mac.

When a soldier decides to leave the army in all their wisdom extract all the work they can out of him, regardless of past conduct. Me and Mac were no exception. A few months before we were due to depart to civilian street we were moved in to a transit block. This is done for two reasons. Firstly, so the departing soldier won't influence his colleagues to join him and secondly when there are any shitty jobs to be done, it is the transit block full of potential civvies they turn to.

The person in charge of these work parties is the Regimental provo sergeant. He also moonlights as the local slave driver. Ours came in the shape of Sergeant Partington. He was all of five feet nothing but had the growl of a rhino and eyes a snake would kill for. He managed to be everywhere at once and he could spot a cigarette end from a thousand meters away. His traditional greeting was "Where the fuck have you been, you twat?" Even if you had just spoken to him five minutes before. There was no escaping from him. I often contemplated sticking one on him, but it was just a pipe dream.

I was to leave a few weeks before Mac and the day of my departure finally arrived. I was apprehensive if not scared. I felt like saying 'can we call this off?' I also knew, deep down, that I had made a mistake. The lads all said their goodbyes and wished me luck. Mac waved at me as I strolled towards the gate.

"Give me a ring in two weeks," he shouted. As I passed the guardroom on my way out Sergeant Partington appeared.

"Good luck, son," he shouted. All my hate for him evaporated. But it made me feel worse, because I realised that he, like most of them, were only doing their jobs at the end of the day.

"Thanks," I replied. I walked out of the gate. I was a civilian and I hated it already.

The first few weeks at home were awful. I was like a fish out of water. I was bored and at a loss as to what to do with myself. Already my father was beginning to irritate me with his petty rules. Only my younger sister Mary was still at home and I think I was infringing on her territory. We had our first argument within a few weeks of me arriving home. I still felt as if I had a black cloud over me.

It wasn't long before my final pay cheque from the Army ran out so I began looking for work, without success. On the spur of the moment I telephoned Cadbury's. I had an interview that week and they offered me my old job back. I reasoned that, as much as I had hated it the first time I was there, I needed the money so I had no option.

One hot summer's day I walked into work reached the changing rooms, and sat down in despair. I hated the place more than I had the first time. I had nothing in common with the people I was working with. I think they must have thought I was on another planet.

"Fuck this!" I said to anyone who happened to be listening and I walked out. I was now very much in the shit with my father and I felt like I had out-stayed my welcome. It was all so very different from the year before when I had been welcomed back as the conquering hero. The final straw came a few weeks later after yet another drunken night out. I left some food on the cooker and nearly burned the house down. It was time to go. I ended up dossing down on my sister's settee. My family must have been bitterly disappointed in me. They thought I had gone mad. In between all this mayhem I was still making visits to Sarah who at the time was totally unaware of my predicament. After a few weeks as a temporary lodger at my sister's I managed to lobby the local council in to letting me a flat. I moved in with just a cooker and a bed. I had managed to get the odd few days a week on building sites to fund my nightly excursions to the pub.

As the months rolled by, I passed the stage of caring. I had stopped making excuses to Sarah for failing to make dates. I simply wouldn't turn up. I rang her after another night drinking and received the full wrath of her mother's anger. She made it clear that my relationship with her daughter was hanging by a thread and it would be better for all concerned if I left her alone and moved on.

It seemed like I had fallen out with just about everyone. But I blamed them. I never once considered that it was something I had done. Not for one second did I think it might have anything to do with my own attitude. One night I walked in to the local pub I spotted my sister Mary with a few of her mates and one of my mates, although we weren't close. I was incensed that he hadn't come over to say hello and my sister completely ignored me. I sat down with my pint of beer. As I did so they all began laughing and joking. I couldn't contain my anger anymore. I picked up the still full pint of beer marched over to my sister and threw the contents at her with all the strength I could muster. A look of horror registered on her face a second before the wall of beer hit her. As I spun round I could hear the gasps of shock as it dawned on people what had just happened. I felt no satisfaction at what I had just done. In fact, I regretted it immediately.

That night I drifted from pub to pub and got steadily pissed and eventually I returned to my flat. I had just slumped on the bed when there was a loud banging on the front door. I staggered up and opened it to be met by two policemen, a sergeant and a constable.

"May we come in?" asked the sergeant as he brushed past me. I followed them into the bedroom. "Sit down, Edward, sit down," said the Sergeant

"I don't want to si . . ."

"Sit down! Now!" boomed the sergeant with a voice of authority I hadn't heard since leaving the army. He was a big bastard and I was under no illusion as to what would happen if I didn't do as I was told. "Look son," said the sergeant in a softer voice which took me by surprise. "You know why we are here, don't you?"

"The pint?" I replied. He nodded

"Yes, and we know all about you just coming back from

the Falklands. Look, Eddy, we all suffer stress at some stage. If you feel you should talk to someone go and do it. Don't feel embarrassed."

"Okay, I'm sorry," I said.

"It's your sister you should apologise to, not us. Go and sort this out," replied the policeman. The police left and I lay there wondering what had gone wrong in my life.

I took the policeman's advice and made it up with my sister. But I continued on my path of self-destruction. On a weekend visit to Mac's we were getting some food from the local takeaway after a night out when I felt something splash over me. It turned out to be coke. When we went outside the lad who had the coke was standing there laughing, so I hit him. A few weeks later I was fined £70 for my actions.

Sarah turned up at the flat one night and gave me the news I was expecting.

"We are finished," she announced. I held myself together until she had gone then I broke down. I knew it was all my own fault, but it made it no easier.

Mates I could count on when I was the hero returning from the Falklands were no longer calling to see me now I really needed them. I ached inside from my split with Sarah and I knew I had to do something to sort my life out. At one point I even decided to join the French Foreign Legion. I went as far as going to Paris but I didn't have the nerve to go through with it and returned home.

My mate Mick came home on a weekend's leave and he was giving me all the banter from the regiment. The regiment was now back in Dortmund, Germany and my old battery had converted to the new self propelled Rapier system which could fire eight missiles. And being on tracks it was very manoeuvreable. It was altogether more advanced.

"Ed, why don't you come back in to the regiment?" Mick kept bringing it up all weekend and the more I thought about it the more I realised that it was the answer to all my problems. By the time Mick had gone back I had made my mind up to at least try. My life was in a mess so I had nothing to lose.

I rang the army careers office and explained that I had already served three years and basically would they consider taking me back? I thought the guy on the other end of the phone was going to tell me to 'fuck off' but he was as nice as pie. I walked in to the army careers office the following day.

"You the re-enlistment?" asked the recruiting sergeant with a smile.

"Yes", I replied. I was obviously not as green looking as the lads sitting around the office. "Right, mate, let's start the ball rolling. Would you like a coffee?" asked the sergeant.

"I'd love one," I replied. This was all so different from the first time I had joined.

This was a turning point in my life. I now had a purpose and instead of boozing I began to get fit. My only concern was that the army would turn me down at some stage, but it was a slow process and all I could do was wait. I told my family of my plans and they were delighted. Delighted to see the back of me or delighted that was getting my life together, I wasn't sure.

During my wait to re-enlist, my sister Twink and I decided to do a parachute jump for a worthy cause, namely the special care baby unit at our local hospital, Arrowe Park. One of my mates, Ray liked the idea and decided to join us. We travelled to Blackpool where we were going to complete the jump. I have always had a fear of heights but I tried to hide it. We spent a full day training ready to jump that evening. The training was good and it helped ease my fears a bit. We went through all the emergency drills, including parachute failure! The day passed quickly and in no time we were out on the runway boarding the tiny Cessna aircraft we would jump from. Trussed up in our parachutes we were helped aboard.

I was last on which meant I was to be first out. I wasn't too happy with this arrangement. I wanted to see it work before I jumped.

The plane rolled down the runway with its engine screaming and me holding on for grim death. It suddenly made a leap and we were airborne. I was not at all happy. I couldn't help but look down at the scene below me and I felt sick. Blackpool's famous Tower looked tiny. I glanced back at my sister and my mate for some reassurance. They had lost all their composure. The look of utter fear on their faces betrayed their true feelings. The instructor indicated to me to put my legs out of the door. As soon as I did so I could feel the wind trying to drag me out. All too soon the engine spluttered to a near stall which meant my departure from the aircraft was imminent. My heart went into my mouth. We had reached 2,500 feet. The instructor held my shoulder and gave me a smile. I replied with a weak grin. I couldn't even pretend that I wasn't scared. GO! I felt the smack on my back. I leapt out of the door with all the strength I could muster. My eyes were firmly closed, I seemed to be falling forever. I had the sensation that I was falling upside down and spinning. For a moment I had the feeling I had jumped to my death. I opened my eyes and looked up just in time to see my parachute inflate into a perfect circle. I felt elated. It was so quiet. I could see far out over the Irish sea. All this was very short lived, however. I had an appointment with the ground which was looming up to meet me fast. I landed with a thump and I was way off target, but I hadn't broke any bones. I was very happy.

We delivered our £300 sponsor money to the hospital a few weeks later and the nurses kindly showed us where the money was to be spent. It was heart breaking to see the tiny babies, looking so fragile.

The letter I had been waiting for from the army finally arrived. I tore open the envelope with trepidation. What if I have been refused and they wouldn't have me back? I tore open the envelope and saw the words 'Report Woolwich'. I whooped with delight. I was back in. On the day I was to report back to the training depot at Woolwich I handed the keys of my flat back to the council. I said all my goodbyes and boarded the train for London. I felt I had turned a corner on a particularly unhappy period of my life. My thoughts turned to Sarah. It was over between us and there was no turning back, but I felt saddened that she wouldn't know I was back in the army. I pushed her to the back of my mind and looked to the future. I was on my own again with all my worldly possessions stuffed into one small holdall, but I felt confident I would be all right. I would make sure.

8

The train pulled in at Woolwich station. The tannoy echoed the words 'Mind the gap.' I made my way up the familiar steps of Woolwich station and out into the town centre. There was no one to meet me this time, that little privilege is reserved for raw recruits. The barracks are situated about a mile or so from the station and all of it is up hill. I didn't have enough money to take a taxi so I started to walk. It was now I began to have serious doubts as to whether I had made the right decision by re-enlisting. The nearer I got to the camp the more I began to panic. I eventually arrived at the guardroom sweating buckets from my walk.

"Can I help you?" barked the sergeant from behind the plate glass window of the guardroom. "Yes," I replied, "I am re-enlistment Gunner Denmark." The bombardier who was sitting next to the sergeant picked up the phone. After a brief conversation, in which I heard my name mentioned, he put the phone down and told me to follow a soldier who had just appeared out of the guardroom. I was lead through to headquarters and the civilian offices.

One of the civvy staff took all my details and I was led upstairs to the battery sergeant major's office. As we ascended the steps up to his office, the familiar smell of army polish used on the gleaming floors hit me. The soldier who was accompanying me tapped timidly on the BSM's door.

"Yes," came the reply from within. The soldier popped his head round the door.

"Sir, Gunner Denmark is outside"

"Okay, send him in," I heard the BSM say.

"Okay mate," whispered the soldier as I was dressed in civilian clothes. I walked in and stood at ease in front of him. He looked smart as all BSMs do, but he had that edge of sharpness about him which is required of anyone serving in a training depot regardless of rank. He looked up at me and then began studying the file in front of him, a file with my name emblazoned across it. Without looking up he began to speak.

"Ahh, Gunner Denmark, you have picked up some bad habits since you left the army haven't you?" My mind was racing, *what* bad habits? Did he think I had been taking drugs? Had one of my family written to him and spilled the beans on my exploits while I had been out?

"Haven't you?" he said again, prompting me for an answer. "Yes, sir," I replied thinking 'fuck it, plead guilty, don't annoy him.'

"Yes", he said echoing my reply "And do you know what bad habit I am referring to?"

How many were there? Oh fuck, I'm cornered! "No, sir," I spluttered.

"Stand to attention," he screamed. I leapt into the air with fright and landed rigidly to attention. "That bad habit," he said in a much calmer voice.

It was decided that I would complete a driving course, then fly out to Dortmund and rejoin 'T' Battery. In the mean time I moved into my accommodation block with the guys who were on the driving course. They had just completed their basic training and once they had finished the driving course they would be sent to their various units. I felt strange to be amongst these recruits who were still wet behind the ears. They had no concept of what it would be like in a front line regiment and it was pointless me trying to explain. They would have to find out for themselves, like I did. One of them was going to 'T' Battery, so I took him under my wing. He was a nice lad but he lacked the sense of urgency required of soldiers. It would take him forever to press his uniform or bull his boots and although this wasn't a big problem it would land him in trouble once he got to 'T' Battery. His name was Ramsey but he reminded me of a character out of the Scooby Doo cartoon so I christened him Shaggy. The name stuck throughout his time in the army. I even heard sergeant majors shouting Shaggy!

Some of the new boys were mouthy and I could not be bothered to try and explain that if they still had this attitude once they arrived at their regiments then they would have it knocked out of them. One guy in particular stood out as a bully amongst them and he was in my room along with four others. A quick chat with Shaggy confirmed that the bully Gunner Naylor was indeed the one who had called all the shots during their basic training. I knew it was only a matter of time before we clashed. He kept his distance at first, eyeing me with suspicion.

Returning from the NAAFI one night with Shaggy we heard laughter as we approached the accommodation block. I sensed something was afoot. I opened the door and walked into the room. A poster I had put up above my bed was on the floor ripped to shreds, along with my mattress and bedding. None of the boys in the room spoke.

"Who's fucking done this?" I screamed.

"Don't know," muttered a few of them under their breath. Naylor wasn't in the room, but I already knew he would be involved. I realised that I wasn't going to get a confession by asking so I ran to the end of the room and picked up a lad by the scruff of his collar and pushed him up against his locker and drew my fist back as if to punch him.

"Naylor!" he screamed, "it was Naylor! You can ask them!" I looked round the room, they all nodded.

"It was Naylor," they confirmed.

"Where is he?" I asked.

"He's at the guardroom," replied the lad I still had pinned up against his locker. "He's in his best uniform because he failed his inspection this morning."

I didn't bother tidying the mess up. I sat down and waited for Naylor to return. I didn't wait long . The noise of him clumping up the stairs in his best boots echoed round the block. The door swung open and in strolled Naylor as bold as brass.

"The wankers!" he protested. "I have to go back to the guardroom because they found some fluff on my hat."

"Naylor!" I shouted "Did you do this to my bed?"

"Not me, sunshine," he replied without even looking at me. I leapt off the bed and launched myself at him. Hearing the commotion he swung round. I threw him against the wall and smacked him in the face. He crumpled up on the floor

"Sorry, Scouse, sorry!" he kept bleating.

"You ever touch anything of mine again and I will kill you!" I screamed. He picked himself up and tried to straighten his jacket and shirt from where I had swung him round. It was a waste of time because he had a blue streak of paint on his back where he had hit the wall. "I'm in the shit now," he blubbered when one of the lads pointed it out. Naylor made his way to the guardroom only to return a few minutes later with instructions for me to report there. I made my way over knowing that Naylor would have been economical with the truth to save his own arse. I stopped in front of the guardroom window and it slid open.

"You are?" asked the duty sergeant.

"Gunner Denmark, sergeant," I replied.

"Gunner Denmark why has Gunner Naylor got paint on his jacket and a swollen lip?" I explained to the sergeant what Naylor had done and told him exactly what Naylor had said when I had questioned him about it. I fully expected to be marched at the double into the cell behind the guardroom.

"Okay, come with me," said the sergeant and off we went towards my room. "I know you have been in the army before," he said on the way over, "so I won't talk to you like a recruit, but I have got to find out what's gone on." When we reached the block I was ordered to wait outside while the sergeant went inside. A few seconds later Naylor came outside smirking.

"He's asking them what happened," he said, "and then you are in the shit."

"If I am Naylor," I replied, "I will make sure you get the good hiding you deserve." I was now feeling a bit concerned. Would the boys back Naylor up if they were in fear of him? The door opened and the sergeant came bursting out. He came straight over to me and put his face close to mine.

"Next time you hit him do it harder, you hear me!"

"Yes, sergeant," I replied finding it hard to hide my relief.

"Naylor! Get your arse over to the guardroom NOW," he screamed. Naylor came back to the room later that night looking completely knackerd but never said a word. I could tell by his looks that we were never going to be friends.

One week before leave I was summoned to the BSM's office. I walked in and stood to attention.

"Good lad, stand at ease," he said "Right, Denmark, after Christmas leave you will be going straight over to Germany to rejoin 12 Regiment. Okay, son?"

"Yes, sir," I replied. I felt elated to be getting away from the training depot. "Unfortunately, Gunner Denmark," he added "there is a battle fitness test tomorrow and let me warn you that a certain officer will be monitoring your efforts so be warned."

"Okay, sir, thanks," I replied, "I'll make the effort."

The following morning we were lined up ready for the BFT

which consists of running in a squad and then completing 1 ½ miles individually. I was apprehensive only because I was being watched. Shaggy pointed to the lad in front.

"See him," he said, "he's like shit off a shovel! He always comes first." The lad certainly had the right build being tall and lean. We set off as a squad. This was the easy bit. I had kept myself fit so I had no worries about not finishing, but I did want to finish in a respectable place. We passed the 1 ½ mile stage and stopped.

"Right, I want a good effort!" boomed the instructor. I put my head down and set off. Once I had got into my pace, I began to pass more and more people until there was only one person in front of me. It was Shit-off-a-Shovel. Something inside me clicked and I went into overdrive, I flew past him. I could see the instructor and so I kept going. Unbelievably I came in first. The BSM came over to me smiling.

"Denmark, you twat, why didn't you tell me you could run? Well done," he said patting me on the back.

"I don't like to boast, Sir," I replied smugly.

Waiting at Woolwich train station ready to go on Christmas leave I caught sight of Naylor on the opposite platform. He saw me and looked away so I left it at that. A few moments later his train drew into the station. Once Naylor was securely seated he began to stare at me through the window and as soon as the train began to pull out he stood up and shouted obscenities through the window. I always wished I would catch up with Naylor, but I never did.

Christmas leave was wonderful, for the first time in a few years I had money in my pocket and Mick was himself on leave from 12 Regiment. Mick gave me the low down on who was still in the regiment and who had left. Surprisingly a lot of my old colleagues were still there. I was a bit worried as to what type of reception I would get. Would the lads look on me as a failure for re-enlisting? It wasn't long before I was to find out.

After flying out to Dusseldorf airport, I was picked up in a Landrover and taken to 12 Regiment in Dortmund. I didn't know the driver but he knew who I was, and told me that all the lads knew I was on my way back. We pulled up outside the T Battery office. I had been ordered to report to the BSM. I knocked nervously on his door

"Yes come in," shouted a voice. I walked in and stood to attention in front of BSM Fenton's desk. "Aah, Denmark," he smirked, "welcome back to 12. You loved us so much you had to come back."

"Near enough, sir," I replied.

"Welcome back," he repeated. "You are aware that we now operate tracked Rapier aren't you?"

"Yes Sir," I replied.

"Okay, you will be in Sergeant Henwood's crew again." This pleased me because I knew Geordie Henwood well having served with him in the Falklands.

The next few weeks were spent settling in and getting familiar with tracked Rapier. Apart from this new equipment not much had changed. I met up with colleagues I had not seen for a while. A lot of them seemed totally fed up and there was talk of wanting to leave. Although I respected their decisions I did warn them to think hard about it. I did not want them making the same mistake as I had done. I completed another signals course, the reason being that the regiment was now using a new burst transmission device which was introduced during my absence. I was very impressed with it, the most longwinded message could be sent out at the push of a button.

Mac had already told me of his intention to re-enlist while I was at Woolwich. But I got a shock when I walked into my room after a trip to the NAAFI and he was sitting on my bed. We went down town and got drunk as skunks. As the months rolled by I got into the routine of exercises and guard duties. Although I was happy I could see the potential for me becoming bored again, until I met up with an old mate in the cookhouse. I was expressing my fears to him of becoming stale and disillusioned.

"Well, Scouse, why don't you apply to 'P' Company?" he said.

"'P' Company?" I said puzzled.

"Yes," he went on "'P' Company Paratrooper course. It's one of the most physically challenging courses in the Army, but if you pass you can join 7th Royal Horse Artillery (7 RHA) which is an airborne regiment in support of the parachute regiment."

The seed was planted, I put my application in the following week and began to get even fitter. In the meantime we were about to embark on a big exercise in a place called Soltau which is around 80 miles from Hamburg. Soltau is the pits: cold, muddy, desolate and devoid of life. It's a huge training area perfect for the army.

The day before we were due to move to Soltau I was in my room preparing my kit when one of the full screws (bombardier), Brian Spence, walked in. He was smiling which is a dead give away that there is a crap job about to be handed out.

"Oh fuck, please don't tell me Brian. What crap have I got?" I moaned.

"It's not just you, Scouse," Brian said, "it's both of us. We've got to get pen and paper and go round the battery and ask for the lads comments on the food in the cookhouse."

"Piss off, Brian, you are winding me up!" I yelled.

"Scouse, I'm telling you the truth. We've got to report to the master chef at 3 pm today with their comments." It was accepted by all the soldiers that the cookhouse food was the pits. In fact it was inedible and that the reason the majority of the lads chose to eat out at their own expense, despite the fact that the money for the meals they did not or could not eat was deducted from their pay each month.

Armed with our pen and paper, Brian and I set about getting the lads comments. After they had finished laughing and realised we were serious, the universal reply was, "it's shit." Brian and I pointed out that these types of comment would not be acceptable to the master chef and so could we have some constructive criticism please. 'The food is never cooked.' 'The food is cold.' It went on and on. Brian and I duly logged what the lads had to say and at the appointed time we reported to the cookhouse.

The master chef and his subordinates were sat around a table drinking tea.

"Sit down," he snorted. "Right, let me hear your comments." Brian nudged me under the table. I cleared my throat.

"The main complaint, sir," I said, "is that the food is not cooked and . . ."

"I don't want to hear that!" the Master Chef shouted. "Just tell me what they think."

"They think the food is bad sir," I said holding back from saying it was shite. The colour drained from his face. He spluttered for words.

"How dare you say that. Our food is the best. Now piss off and tell them bastards over at the accommodation." We informed the lads of the Master Chefs comments. Nobody expected anything else.

The battery trundled down to the railway siding in the tracked Rapiers, where we would load on to German flat car trains for the journey to Soltau. As we were low priority to other trains the move was long and tedious. We arrived in Soltau and unloaded all the Rapiers and support vehicles and moved to the old Nissan huts where we would spend a few days before moving out on to the exercise area proper. I didn't expect the accommodation to be the Ritz, but it was poor even by army standards. The concrete floor was covered in mud. There was the odd bed without any mattresses but, above all, it was freezing and the little gas stoves had been removed and taken to the officers' quarters. That night I drifted in and out of sleep to the sound of teeth chattering. I could hear rats scurrying around in the dark.

The following morning we began preparing the Rapiers for the exercise. Only half the troop would be going out and I was one of the unlucky ones. It was so cold we even ate our dinner in an old toilet block that reeked of shit. The exercise was a pain in the arse from start to finish, we were enemy against main battle tanks. These huge monsters were much faster than us so we really stood no chance. It was rather like a cat playing with a mouse, and on this occasion we were the mouse. Once the tanks had had their fun we moved back to the Nissan huts. The other lads we left behind were far more happy. They had been on fatigues while we had been away. Mac came strolling over grinning from ear to ear.

"Scouse, you tosser, have you missed me?"

"Fuck off, Mac," I replied.

"Scouse," he went on ignoring my insult, "guess what? We're all going on the piss in Hamburg." I had heard rumours that we might get a night off and we had been told to take civvy clothes with us, but it was far from certain.

That night we all climbed on to the back of the army four ton wagon reeking of a cocktail of aftershaves. The BSM stood watching us and he took the opportunity to give us a stern warning not to miss the wagon or be late getting back. We were ordered to be back at the four ton wagon at one AM. It would drop us off on the outskirts of Hamburg. For some unknown reason military vehicles were not permitted in to the city itself. I had been to Hamburg once before, so I knew my way round a bit. As soon as the wagon drew to a halt we spilled out, everyone moving off in different directions, me and Mac headed for the infamous Reeperbahn. After a few drinks we decided to sample the seedier parts.

One grotty bar had the words LIVE SEX SHOW over the door. This will do we both agreed. We descended some steps into a dimly lit cellar. There was a small bar with an old woman standing behind it holding a mangy dog.

"Come, come, welcome," she beckoned. On the far wall an old projector was playing an equally old film of a woman stripping. This was the live sex show. As my eyes adjusted to the light I could just make out a bunch of old men seated in the corner who were so transfixed on the film that they were not even aware of us. Mac looked at me.

"Fuck this," we said in unison. As we turned to leave the old woman began shouting

"Nein, nein! Come, come!" Realising that we were leaving despite her pleas, she let out a string of obscenities. As we made our way back up the stairs she threw the mangy dog to the floor. It chased after us snapping and barking. We rolled back on to the street laughing. "Mac," I said, "lets just go and get pissed."

After visiting our fourth bar we were quite smashed. Around midnight we started to make our way back to the wagon, meeting up with the other lads as we went. Everyone was pissed off because we were just starting to warm up. We reluctantly climbed on to the back of the wagon.

"This is ridiculous," Mac protested, "we could have stayed a few more hours."

"I know Mac," I said, "back to that shithole to freeze our bollocks off." As the last stragglers climbed in Mac started laughing. "What the fuck's up with you?" I said.

"Do you fancy jumping back off and staying in Hamburg for the night?" Mac said still grinning.

"We will be in for the high jump when we get back tomorrow," I replied.

"Who gives a shit," said Mac as he leapt off the back of the wagon. I thought about the consequences of what we were doing for about a second and followed him. We were truly in the shit. There were a lot of two-faced bombardiers on the back of the wagon who would run and tell the battery sergeant major as soon as the wagon returned to Soltau minus Mac and me.

We headed back for the bright lights of Hamburg giggling like a couple of school girls at our prank. We had drunk too much beer to fully appreciate what we had done. At some point in the night my brain ceased to function under the tide of alcohol I had consumed. I forced my eyes to open and then I was hit by a wave of nausea and the mother of all headaches. I heaved myself in to a sitting position and took stock of my surroundings. I was in a shop doorway still in Hamburg, frozen solid. Mac was sprawled out about a foot away. I shuffled over and kicked him awake, he mumbled and moaned.

"Oh fuck, me head," he moaned. It all came thundering home to me like an express train. "Oh shit", Mac groaned.

We pooled our money together in the hope we would have enough to get back to Soltau and the punishment that would be awaiting us. No such luck. We had enough to buy a cup of coffee and to make it part of the way by train. We looked like a couple of tramps as we set off. I knew a small type of car train ran through to Soltau but the station it ran from was many miles away. We had been walking for hours when we ended up in a forest. I was sure we were going in the right direction.

"Mac I need a piss, hold on," I shouted.

"Me, too," he replied. We both stood there relieving ourselves against a tree discussing the punishment we would receive, when for some reason, I looked round and no more than a hundred feet away was a German shepherd running towards us in attack mode baring its fangs. Without even putting myself away I sprang up the tree. I had no time to warn Mac apart from a scream but he had by instinct realised

I wasn't fooling about and was right behind me. The dog stood at the base of the tree barking furiously.

"Mac, what the fuck are we going to do?" I said

"This is getting ridiculous," replied Mac. "Where's it's owner?".

Then we heard a whistle from within the forest and the dog bounded away wagging its tail. To be on the safe side we remained up the tree for the best part of an hour.

Just before dinnertime we found the station, paid our fare, and boarded the train. We fell in to our seats.

"Ed, Ed, wake up there's the Nissan huts and the lads," screamed Mac. And sure enough we could see them all.

"Stop! Halt!" I shouted at the driver. "Oh, fuck Mac, where's the next station. We are going to be lost again." But our luck was in. The train began to slow and then it pulled into a station about a mile from where we had seen the lads.

As we began the walk back to the camp we put our story together. We would say Mac had left his coat, so he jumped off the wagon to retrieve it and I went along to make sure he was okay. The lads' mouths dropped as we walked back into the camp.

"You two are in the shit! The BSM is going mad!"

Eventually we arrived at the BSM's office. I tapped on the door and it swung open. Not only was the BSM at his desk, all the troop's sergeants and officers were in there. At the sight of Mac and I they began to snigger. We had the appearance of a couple of tramps who had just survived a bus crash.

"You fucking clowns!" screamed the BSM, "where have you been?" Mac went into the story about losing his coat. The BSM then looked at me and said, "I suppose you went along to hold his hand did you Denmark?" I put on a hurt look.

"He is my mate, sir. I couldn't leave him to go back by

himself." This went down well with the BSM and he calmed down.

"Okay," he relented. "How the fuck did you get back." We told him about the train and the walk we had done.

"I can't let this go unpunished," he said, "so you are both on fatigues today and you will be on gardening when we get back to Dortmund." I was elated we had got off so lightly and amazed that no one had spilled the beans on us.

Back in Dortmund I received notice that I had been accepted by the Paras. Mac had also applied, but had heard nothing and it seemed likely that his application was never forwarded to the Paras. It was a blow for me because it would have been better to have a mate to help each other but this was the type of cock-up we had to put up with. The "Chairborne Infantry" who ran the regiment did not give a shit and as a result Mac missed out on a chance to gain a red beret.

I was due to report to Aldershot in three weeks, but I was about to go skiing for two weeks, so it would mean I would only have a week to sort my kit out before leaving. The course programme I was given had a list of things I would need: PT vest, lightweight trousers, plasters, talc strapping etc. It gave me a clear indication that this was not going to be easy. The form was I would spend three weeks at 7 Royal Horse Artillery on a pre Para selection course. This by all accounts was a grueller and its purpose was to get rid of all the dead wood, i.e. those people who were just not fit enough and did not stand much chance of passing P company, be it through attitude or fitness or if your face did not fit with the instructor. Pre-Para would sort out the men from the boys. I used my two weeks skiing course to bring myself to nearly my peak of fitness. I would ski all day, come in off the slopes, get changed and go running. The deep snow covered hills of Baveria proved to be excellent for improving my stamina. On one or two occasions a couple of the lads came with me, I had left them behind after the first quarter mile and I had showered changed and had dinner before they had returned. I was certainly fit, but would I be fit enough?

9

On my return to Dortmund from Bavaria, I began packing my kit. I had a flight booked for the following day. I had managed to get a couple of days leave before reporting to 7 RHA at Aldershot. It felt sad saying goodbye to my mates and odd because if I was to see them again it would mean I had failed. Mac by this time had managed to get himself on a Northern Ireland tour with another regiment, though he was only still training. It sounded exciting. He would come back to the room each evening with tales of what he had been doing. I began to wonder if I had made the right decision. I had always wanted to serve in Northern Ireland, because I had heard so much about it. My own brother, Pete, had served there during his time in the army, but it looked as though I had missed my chance.

The following morning my transport arrived to take me to the airport.

"See you round then, Mac," I said, "keep your head down over there." He grinned and said "Best of luck, Ed." We were both gutted that we were not on the course together.

I spent my few days leave at home just resting and basically worrying about what lay ahead. All too soon I was on the train heading for Aldershot. When the train eventually pulled in I felt sick. I had the urge to get back on the next train out and go back to Germany. I got a taxi up to Lille Barracks where 7 RHA are based.

"On 'pre-para' are we mate?" said the taxi driver. "Er . . . yes," I replied, taken aback by his knowledge.

"The first day's the worst" he went on. "Are you ex-para?" I asked.

"No, no," he said, shaking his head, "I just run them up here and when they fail I take them back," he said laughing at his own joke. "See ya, then," he said sniggering as I got out.

I walked over to the guardroom.

"Gunner Denmark," I said to the Sentry, "I'm on pre-para."

"Fuck off now," he said "while you can still go! And book in at the window," he added. It was too late to turn back now. I was shown to the accommodation block where I and the rest of the low-life pre-para candidates would be living. It was on a par with the transit wing at Woolwich. That is to say it was a shithole. I was issued with bedding by a stony faced storeman who only grunted the words 'sign here' throughout the whole procedure. I shuffled down the corridor under my bedding.

"In 'ere," the storeman pointed to a room. He then disappeared off down the corridor. I pushed the door open with my bedding and went in. There were eight beds and only one of them was taken, this by a lad who was fast asleep. I moved to the far end of the room and plonked my gear onto a bed in the corner. I had learned very early in the army that it is unwise to sleep by the door, the reason being that if an NCO wants a soldier for fatigues then he will simply open the door and nominate the first person he sees. As I was unpacking and making my bed up, the sleeping beauty a couple of beds away began to stir.

"All right, mate," I shouted trying to make conversation, and more importantly see if I could get some information off him.

"Ay," he replied.

"Are you on the course tomorrow?" I asked him trying to coax some words out of him.

"Ay," he replied again. "I was on the last pre-para course, but I hurt my ankle so I was back-squadded." At last I was getting somewhere.

"What's it like?"

"It's fucking hard," he said as he walked out the door. I made up my mind that I would have to find out for myself.

Over the next few hours the other pre-para recruits began to arrive. A tall blonde athletic looking lad took the bed next to mine.

"All right, mate," he said, and introduced himself. His name was Gavin and he was a military policeman. As the conversation went on I came to realise that poor Gavin did not have a clue as to what he had let himself in for. I was in the dark as to what the routine would be, but at least I knew it was going to be painful. Gavin had been told by his boss, himself a Para, that P Company was a walk in the park. He had been set up, but I did not have the heart to tell him.

At six the next morning the words echoed around the accommodation block. "Outside!" We all ran out and formed into three ranks. Four Paras stood there, their eyes scanning the rows of men. A Para officer stepped forward.

"The dress gentlemen, is boots, lightweights, red PT vest. So you five fuck off and get changed," he shouted to the five unlucky recruits wearing white PT vests. "The dress in the afternoon will be PT vest, shorts and pumps. I advise you to read orders here or you will be returned to the unit RTU'ed." We were then marched over to the stores and issued with webbing and Bergens. After assembling our webbing we were ordered to fall in again outside the block. The Para officer once again addressed us. "Gentlemen, there are about forty recruits standing here, by tomorrow at least ten of you will be on your way back to your units, and this is pre-para not P company."

We were divided into three sections although this part of the course was run by the Royal Horse Artillery. There were soldiers from many different regiments here. Gavin was in my section and a lad I had met the previous night called Clarke. Clarkey, as he was called, was on his second attempt. He had completed the whole course including 'P' company but had failed due to his attitude. I could see why. He was so laid-back nothing bothered him and in the eyes of the training staff he was coasting and not giving it a 100%. I liked Clarkey, I also liked his attitude. Besides that he let me know what we were in for.

The first few runs we would do without webbing and Bergens, but as the course progressed then so would the weight we carried in our Bergens. The more I asked Clarkey, the more I worried, so I decided to let things happen. We set off on our first run. It was quite enjoyable, fast but rather nice. One or two of the boys were running into trouble already, one of them being Gavin. We had already been warned not to leave people behind, so Clarkey and I got hold of Gavin and dragged him along. I think the awful truth was now beginning to dawn on him, and this was only the morning of day one. We had only covered about three miles when Gavin started to go down, his eyes were rolling to the back of his head and froth was coming out of his mouth. I thought he was having a fit.

"Staff!" I yelled to one of the Paras.

"Is he all right?"

"Let go of him," he replied. I was only to glad too do so, my own energy was ebbing away pushing such a dead weight. As soon as Clarkey and I let go, Gavin slumped to the floor. The last I saw of him was as he was being bundled into the back of a Landrover. We pressed on and although it was tiring it was okay.

We returned to barracks just before dinner to find Gavin's bed space empty. I looked at Clarkey and seeing the look on my face he laughed.

"Get used to it and be thankful it's not you. They get shut of failures fast so they don't rub off on the rest." We all ran over to the cookhouse for dinner. (Walking was not permitted unless medically excused).

"It's not too bad." I said to Clarkey.

"Don't get too confident," he replied "The pressure will really go on this afternoon. They get rid of the slack in stages. Some fucked off this morning, but more will go after today."

That afternoon we set off on our second run of the day. The pace was much faster, interspersed with a series of exercises, push ups, sit ups and sprints. We went on for mile after mile. The three sections were strung out. One or two people were on their knees throwing up. The Para instructors were on anybody who stopped, bawling and yelling. Although I was keeping up, in fact I was doing well, the horrible thought that this was Day One kept coming to me.

"Scouse, it gets better!" shouted Clarkey "Fuck off, Clarke," I replied. We returned to the barracks totally wiped out. A few more had gone in to the Landrover during the afternoon. Once again we returned to empty bed spaces. That night we had an inspection of our rooms. We made the effort to clean and tidy the place but the instructors went crazy. They were shouting threats of throwing the whole room off the course. They put us on bed blocks, something I had not done since basic training and we were re-inspected at midnight. On the stroke of midnight the instructors came barging into the block. I could hear the orders and obscenities even before they had reached our room. I looked across at Clarkey who was squeezing his spots in his locker mirror.

"Clarkey, you bastard, what are you doing?" I whispered.

"Scouse, calm down," he replied nonchalantly. "We'd failed the inspection before they even decided to inspect." A

moment before they entered the room Clarkey closed his
locker spun round and stood at ease. The senior soldier called
the room to attention as they burst in. The four of them went
systematically along the line of beds tipping them over. The
bigger of the four instructors turned on me. I could smell the
alcohol on his breath before he had even started shouting at
me.

"You fucking maggot!" he yelled "Don't you know how
to make a bed block?"

"Yes, Staff," I replied.

"Yes, Staff," he mimicked me. "Well, then," he added,
"why haven't you made one?" I was in a no-win situation,
whatever my reply I was going to get it. "That was the best
I could do, Staff," I replied.

"That fucking heap there is your best effort?" he laughed,
looking at the pile of blankets on the floor.

"It looked a bit better before you threw it on the floor,
Staff," I said. His eyes narrowed. I instantly regretted what
I had said. He moved so close I thought he was going to kiss
me on the lips.

"Are you trying to be funny with me, you piece of shit?"
he said in a low menacing tone.

"No, Staff," I pleaded, "I am sorry. It all came out wrong."

"Good", he said, "because if you are, the first jump you
will make is when I launch you out of that window! Got it!"

"Yes, Staff," I replied. They left the room. We had another
inspection at 1 am. Clarkey fell on the bed laughing. "Scouse,
you knobber! Why the fuck did you say that to him?"

"I don't know," I replied, "it just came out." The next
inspection passed with only the odd threat and we finally fell
into our beds at 2 am. The pain and aching in my limbs as I
got out of bed the next morning was worse than anything
I had before. All my colleagues were in the same state.

"What's up, girls?" mocked one of the instructors as we
fell in outside the block. "Are you all feeling a little bit stiff?"

Author and Family.

Author about to go on patrol.

Rapier Darkfire.

Riot control in Northern Ireland.

The Mob Killing of Corporals Wood's and Howe.

The Mob Killing of Corporals Wood's and Howe.

Enniskillen Bomb 1987.

Scene of the shooting of Breslin and Devine brothers in Strabane by the SAS.

"Yes, staff," we all replied as one. "Well my little darlings, I have some good news for you and some bad news. Which do you want first?" Nobody answered. "Okay," he laughed, "I will give you the good news first. We are going swimming first thing this morning. And now for the bad news. From tomorrow you shall all be carrying 30lb in weight in your Bergens on every run, and I warn you now girls, all your Bergens will be weighed by me before you set off and any bastard found with less than 30lb will have an extra 20lb added on. I don't mind if your Bergens are over 30lb," he added sarcastically. We climbed on to the wagon with the agility of old men and were taken to the pool.

During the journey Clarkey gave me the benefit of his wisdom.

"The best thing to make up the 30lb weight in your Bergen is coke bottles wrapped in towels" he said.

"Why?" I asked perplexed.

"Well," he continued "the staff always weigh the Bergen before a run and never after, so if we are travelling on the wagon anywhere to start a tab(run), if the Landrover that follows gets caught at traffic lights its possible to pour the water from one of the coke bottles, thus reducing the load."

"All well and good," I replied, "but if I get caught it means getting booted off the course."

"Yes," agreed Clarkey, "but life is full of risks." I dismissed the idea. It wasn't worth it. The wagon pulled up at the pool and we climbed out.

"Right, get inside, get changed and be at the poolside in five minutes!" ordered one of the instructors. We all lined up at the edge of the pool. The big Para instructor who had previously threatened to throw me out of the window climbed up on to the diving board still fully clothed. "All those who can't swim raise your hands!" he shouted. The few guys who could not swim reluctantly raised their hands. I could understand their fear, because these sadistic bastards might well force them to jump in the deep end for some fun. The non-swimmers stood there awaiting their fate, but even I was surprised when they were ordered to the shallow end for swimming tuition. The instructor was a female soldier and a pretty one. The sight of big macho soldiers being supported by her while they practised the breast stroke was quite funny. The instructor turned his attention to us.

"Right, I want all you coons to go down one end of the pool while the whites chase you." he said laughing. The few black lads who were on the course did not move an inch. "I'm only joking," said the instructor. If this was a attempt to make them leave the course it had failed because it was like water off a ducks back to them. In all fairness to the instructors, this was a single episode and everyone got the same encouragement, regardless of colour or creed.

All too soon our morning's play in the pool passed and that afternoon we were back to being beasted on yet another tab. I felt quite confident on the runs, but we were running in light order. Carrying Bergens would make a difference. We had already lost a few men even in these early stages. They had left for variety of reasons, some purely because the course was too demanding, others because of injuries. Something as simple as turning an ankle was all it took. So demanding was the course that anything but 100% health and it would be impossible to carry on.

The introduction of carrying Bergens of 30lb was a shock to the system. In my naivete, I imagined that carrying such weight we would slow our pace accordingly. No such luck. The instructors were away like Olympic runners off starting blocks, shouting threats if we did not close up behind them. We would run a good distance then start to force-march. I found the force-marching very hard indeed, it took a lot of practice to get the hang of it and after a while my thighs felt like they were on fire. This was when people's tempers began to fray. If someone was a bit slow, they would get a dig in the back from the person behind.

The pressure continued each night in the form of room inspections and endless shouting for the slightest thing not in place. My every waking moment seemed to be spent either running or sprinting around a gymnasium like a lunatic. Out of the two I preferred the runs, because if we were in the gym it was impossible to rest even for a second. We gathered outside the gym one morning ready to fall in for the normal run when I noticed that there were more instructors joining us than usual. I turned to Clarkey to find out if there was anything ominous about these additional instructors.

"What it means, Scouse," he said with a very worried look on his face, "is that we are in for one bad fucking day!" Much to my horror, he was right.

We followed a route over an armoured vehicle training area. It was full of ditches, which in turn were full of water, sometimes chest deep. But by far the worst was the mud, it was almost impossible to lift my feet. I could feel my strength just ebbing away. My lungs were ready to burst, my throat burned as I frantically tried to suck in air to keep the momentum up. At some point I had stopped moving, I was face down in the mud. It had found its way into every orifice. I could hear people screaming and shouting, but it sounded so far off, and dreamlike I was happy to lie there and go off to sleep. With an almighty thrust I was pulled to my feet by my collar. "Move it cunt, or I will drown you here and now!" screamed the instructor. I used every ounce of strength in my body to propel myself forward out of my muddy grave. I looked over and my glance fell on Clarkey who was trying to crawl his way out of the thick slimy mud. He was so far gone that he did not even register I was there. He had a look of sheer desperation on his face. I fell into a ditch of water. Still moving forward I pulled myself out. The water had washed some of the mud away. Without the dead weight of mud, I was able to make some progress.

"Close up you fucking maggots!" the instructor screamed at us. I closed up behind the lead instructor and in a moment of madness I gripped the back of his Bergen to support myself. Without even bothering to turn round he barked to one of his colleagues "Get this twat off me!" I got a swift well aimed smack to the head. Message received, I let go.

Two more left the course at the end of the day. Back in the room that night we all sat licking our wounds.

"Clarkey, please don't tell me if it's going to be a bad day," I said, sitting down next to him on his bed.

"Fuck off, Scouse," he replied, "why should I suffer alone?"

"Had you lost some money today?" I asked him. "No," he replied, "why?"

"Oh its just that I saw you lying in the mud looking for something."

"You cheeky twat," he replied, "I saw you getting dragged along by the scruff of your neck."

Some of the lads had weird and wonderful methods to treat their blisters, but nothing really worked, including the protective patches I had purchased myself. Once the water had flooded into my boots they fell off. The worst wounds were caused by our Bergens rubbing on our backs. There was no way to prevent this. We all tried cutting foam up and strapping it to the Bergen but it always fell off. All these things had been tried a million times over, but at the end of the day we had to grin and bear it. The instructors did, to their credit give us some good advice. I had to admire them, because they were not resting on their laurels, they carried the same weight as us and completed every task we had to do. Even when we were floundering in the mud they pressed on, their legs like pistons never stopping.

We had paraded outside the gym one morning when

Clarkey and I, along with two others, were told to go and pick the stretcher up from behind the building. Clarkey gave a nervous cough.

"Oh no," I pleaded looking at him, "is it that bad?"

"I'm afraid so," he replied. On lifting the stretcher I began to realise why. It consisted of two long steel tubes filled with concrete and strapped over the top were steel supports. It was so heavy that we had trouble lifting it. We set off on our morning gallop plus stretcher (calling it a stretcher was akin to calling a jumbo jet a glider). Four men carried the stretcher, while the remainder of the section followed behind. When the instructors decided the stretcher bearers were tired, and ready to collapse, the next four in the section would move up and take their place, they in turn would then go to the back of the section moving up and up until they were back on, and so it would continue for mile after mile. Out of all the tasks we had undertaken I found this to be the most traumatic. The second I moved onto the stretcher I wanted to stop. It had to be held at shoulder height but it was impossible to rest it on the shoulder, because had it come in to contact, it would have broken bones. I was using all my willpower and strength to keep going. I kept telling myself the next tree and I will stop. The instructors, seeing when a man was fit to drop, would move in on him and shriek threats of violence into his ear. When I was on the receiving end of this I felt the full brutality of their fury. The sweat was running down from under my helmet and into my eyes. I was running on blind faith that the front men could see. My chest was heaving so much I thought my lungs had burst, but worst of all I could taste blood in the back of my throat. I thought I was going to collapse.

"Keep going, you fucking tosser! Lift the fucking thing up or I will fucking drop you now!" It was my ear the threats were being shouted into. I lifted the stretcher, how I don't know, because I had lost all feeling in my arms. Seeing I had made the effort the instructor moved onto the lad in front, he received the same verbal assault as I had. The next four moved up and took over. It was all I could do to put one foot in front of the other. Grown men were crying, not out of pity for themselves, but because they were pushing their bodies far beyond their own endurance, and that was only possible because of the instructors. Though I did not know it at the time, they knew exactly how far they could push us. I could feel the stretcher rubbing the skin from my shoulder, but it was the pain from my lungs and oxygen starved muscles that hurt the most. My throat was on fire with the effort. The body must produce a natural anaesthetic when pushed to its limit, because I began to feel drunk, the reality of my pain was slipping away. My body was still moving but I was on the very last of my strength and I knew that I was going to collapse at any moment. I would have welcomed it to escape the torture.

Somehow our section reached the gymnasium. There were no dramatics, like soldiers falling to their knees in a state of collapse. It's not the done thing in the Paras. Instead we stood upright sucking in lungs full of air. My head was spinning and I had a raging thirst. I looked round to see how my colleagues had fared, a few of them had not finished with us. As always after a tab, there was an urn full of hot sweet tea. With salt stains round our mouths, we stood waiting impatiently to fill our mugs. This was the best part of the day, but limbs would seize up and it would be an effort to get moving again.

I dragged myself out of bed on the final day of pre-para happy I had got this far but also very concerned because I had developed a cough and during the night I had spat out some blood stained phlegm. Even coughing in front of the Staff would arouse questions of fitness to complete the course. To my utter relief, on parading outside the gym, we were congratulated on getting this far and as it was Friday, we were told we could go home for the weekend, with a stern warning to be ready for P company on the Monday morning. The combination of stiff limbs and blisters must have taken its toll on me, because as I was getting onto the train, an old woman asked me if I could manage. I was tempted to let her carry my bag.

The following day I went to see my own GP, Doctor Janikiewicz. I told him of my chest problem, although I was economical with the truth as to how arduous the course had really been, and the fact that I had spat up blood. In all fairness, I made the course sound like a walk in the park. He prescribed some antibiotics and told me to take things easy.

Sunday night we or rather those of us who were left reported to the Parachute Regiment depot. Clarkey told me, and I believed him, that we would not do anything that much harder than what we had already done, but some of the other lads who had done part or completed P Company, said he was talking crap and that I would see the difference in the morning. A bit later on that night some of the P Company instructors came into the block to give us the once over. Their attitude seemed very different from that of the 'pre Para' staff. They made a few veiled threats as to what we were in for. This also led me to believe that Clarkey was bullshitting me after all.

Monday morning we were marched over to the stores to be issued with helmets and beasting jackets. The jackets were bog standard Army denim jackets that were no longer used except for P Company. Some of the lads who had been on the last course managed to retrieve their old jackets, thus saving them the job of sewing their name tags onto the left breast pocket. After being carried round on a sweaty head for many a course, the helmets stank, so I washed mine in the bath. The whole morning was lost due to administration, so we paraded that afternoon for our first run, surprisingly without our 30lb Bergens. But this was a double- edged sword because, without the weight of the Bergens, we would have to move faster. We were also warned the penalty for any misdemeanour would be having to buy the instructors a jar of coffee and a box of Jaffa cakes. On reflection this was not as easy as it sounded because as was pointed out, at the end of each day a person could be in debt to the tune of a few jars of coffee and biscuits.

We set off on the first run and as predicted it was fast. Apart from my chest I felt the pace was okay. As was the case on most runs, after the first few miles people began to drop back I stayed tucked in behind the lead instructor, but I could hear the slackers getting bawled out and judging by the screams one or two were getting slapped. After what must have been the tenth mile, they started to play games with us. The men from the back would sprint to the front and so on, until we had all done it a dozen times. We carried each other, as you would hold a baby, then we had piggy back races, and finally we leapfrogged each other for mile after mile. I owed two jars of coffee for not making croaking noises whilst leap frogging.

Our route led us off the road through some woods onto a dirt track. We then emerged into a large clearing, where there was a big steel bridge over a canal.

"That's Engineer's Bridge," said Clarkey as he drew breath. "We will have to walk over the top of it," he added. Seeing the fear in my eyes he said, "I am not taking the piss, Scouse, we will have to scale it, then walk over the girders to the other side and climb down." I felt the panic begin to rise in me. I felt sick. I felt scared. Although I had completed a parachute jump this was different. I knew that if I was to slip off this I would surely die. All my fears were confirmed when we were ordered to halt at the bridge.

"What the fuck are you waiting for?" shouted the instructor, "get up there!" The first two men began to climb, then the next two. All the while I was being moved forward. There was no way out. I was trapped. My mind was racing trying to think of a way to stop the inevitable. All too soon it was my turn. I began to climb with all the enthusiasm of a man walking to the gallows. Seeing my apprehension one of the instructors shouted some encouragement.

"Get a move on, before I come up there and throw you off, cunt!"

I reached the top and had to draw on every ounce of courage to stand up from a crouching position. I could not move forward, it was impossible despite the threats being shouted at me from the instructors below.

"Come down now!" one of them screamed up at me. With great care I climbed down. I expected to get the full brunt of the instructor's anger, but he just smirked and told me to go and join the section. Another lad who had also had a crisis of confidence was also told to come down. We arrived back at the gym and we were dismissed, but as I went to walk away I was called back by one of the instructors.

"Denmark, I want a word with you," he said

"Yes, Staff," I replied.

"That was a pretty poor performance on the bridge, don't you think? Well?" he said prompting me to answer.

"I was scared, Staff," I said.

"Go and get in the back of that Landrover," he said in a menacing tone. I walked over to the Landrover wondering what was going to happen to me as I climbed into the back. I could see my fellow vertigo sufferer was already there.

"What's going on?" I asked him "Are we getting thrown off the course?"

"No," he replied, "it's worse than that. They are taking us back to the bridge."

"Oh, fuck no!" I said, "not again." We sat there in the back of the Landrover for about ten minutes, when four of the staff came out of the gym. Two of them got in to the front and two climbed into the back with us.

They never said a word as we drove back to the bridge. I broke out in to a cold sweat. It was a combination of fear and my chest infection.

"Are we going back up the bridge Staff?" I asked the obvious. One of the instructors leaned forward, looking at me.

"You have to overcome your fear, its as simple as that." 'Easy for him' I thought. "Anyway," he added, "the good news is if you slip you will die, but the bad news is you will fail P Company and remain a craphat."

"Out you come girls, its party time!" yelled the driver as we stopped by the dreaded bridge. An instructor placed his hand on my shoulder.

"Look," he said "climb up, walk across and then we can go home for tea, okay? Right up you go then, and don't let me down." Once again I began the climb up the bridge, all the time I kept thinking, 'if I fall I'll fall onto the road or into the canal, and if it's the canal, will it be deep enough to break my fall?' To the casual observer the bridge probably didn't look that high, but for me it was like the Empire State Building, and for every foot I climbed it felt like a hundred. I sat crouching down for a while then I began to stand but once again I lost my nerve and I returned to a crouching position. A volley of abuse and threats came from the instructors below, and to make matters worse the other lad who had also been brought back with me had managed to cross over, his girder ran parallel with mine. "You have got ten seconds to stand up and start walking or I will come up and fucking throw you off. Got it?" shouted one of the instructors. I stood up and began to walk, not because I had found courage, but because I was more in fear that the instructors might carry out their threat. It would be stupid to think for one second that they would throw me onto the road and kill me, but I did think they might throw me into the canal to teach me a lesson, so I carried on and made it to the other side of the bridge. Their anger now turned to praise. I was then made to walk back to the other side. After crossing the bridge a dozen times I was told to come down.

"This bridge holds no fear for you now is that right?" asked the instructor.

"Yes Staff," I lied. We drove back to the barracks for tea but I had no appetite.

Late that night Clarkey returned from one of his nightly adventures and seeing all the 'Sections' green beasting jackets hanging up, he had wrongly assumed that that was what we would be wearing first thing. Wrong! Unknown to him, the programme had changed and we were going to the gym wearing red PT vest, shorts and pumps and not our beasting jackets, which we wore for running only. It was normal practice for the lads to walk round in their undies till the last minute to prevent our immaculately pressed kit from getting creased. As always Clarkey lay in bed until the last minute watching the rest of us rushing around until we began to get dressed. His jaw dropped.

"What the fuck are you doing, Scouse?" he asked

"It's PT, Clarkey, didn't you know, the programme was changed last night."

"Oh fuck!" he yelled. Jumping out of bed, he began to pull his clothes out of the bag he had stuffed them in after being washed and dried. Out came his red PT vest and blue shorts, they resembled a packet of crisps. The lads in the room began to snigger. Clarkeys face drained of colour.

"What the fuck am I going to do? It's too late to iron them."

"Put them on," someone suggested. So he did. He had only himself to blame, but I did feel sorry for him. He was one of the nice guys at the end of the day. The seriousness of the situation was not lost on Clarkey, he was flapping good style.

"Outside now!" came the call from the instructors. We all ran out and formed into three ranks, Clarkey making sure that he was in the rear rank next to me. I was finding it hard to stifle my laughter. Even before the inspection had begun, one of the instructors caught sight of Clarkey. His eyes could not believe what they were seeing. In a moment all the instructors were looking, and most of the section were laughing, but the joke was lost on the instructors. They may have seen it as a challenge to their authority, I don't know. One of them moved round the back of the section and pulled Clarkey out. I heard his PT vest rip. A hush fell over the section. Clarkey was ordered back into the accommodation block, two instructors followed behind him. The inspection went ahead without Clarkey, and to prove a point most of us failed, me because the eyelet's in my pumps were too close together. The lad next to me failed because his eyelets were too far apart. We were put firmly back into place. Because I had not passed the inspection I was put on show clean (i.e. re-inspected). The show clean takes place at 10 o'clock at night, which means staying up for most of the night catching up on pressing kit etc, which should have been done whilst parading.

Clarkey joined us in the gym a bit later on that morning, he had certainly had the wind taken out of his sails.

"What happened?" I asked him out of morbid fascination.

"If I drop another bollock like that I'm off the course," he said.

All the equipment in the gym was made up into a mini assault course and we ran round and round it till we were ragged. I started to feel ill, my chest felt so tight I could not breath. To my utter horror an instructor was concerned enough to ask if I felt okay.

"Yes, Staff," I replied "I just feel a bit shagged out."

"Good, in that case, keep moving," he said. To this day I shall never know how I kept on going, but I did and we eventually finished.

During dinner time I felt so weak I did not get off my bed

let alone eat. All too soon the dreaded call I had been waiting for came echoing up the stairs. "Outside now!"

"Scouse you should go sick." Clarkey advised, "You look like you're fucking dying!"

"Thanks, that's cheered me up." I said, "but I will try and get through this afternoon." Clarkey knew as well as I did that if I was to report sick I would be binned off the course, and then I would have to start from day one 'pre-Para' or go back to 12 Regt. I knew it would have to be the latter, because I could never face doing this ever again.

We formed up into three ranks outside. Our water bottles were checked to see if they were full. If the bottle was anything other than brimming, the offender would have to pour it over his head. Our Bergens were weighed and we were stood at ease and we waited and waited. This was January and we only had a thin layer of clothing on. Half an hour went by, then it began to rain. We stood firm, we had no choice. Someone began to mutter a protest under his breath. All this time the instructors were watching us from their office while they drank coffee. I felt as though I was going to freeze to the spot. The rain continued to fall and we continued our wait. A lad in the front rank moved his arm to wipe the water out of his eyes. The office window flew open and one of the instructors, a black guy shouted the next one to move would be sorry. I found this black instructor to be rather odd. I could not work him out. He didn't shout very often, but if he was unhappy with someone, he could let them know just by looking at them. Personally I was shit scared of him, and so were the rest of the lads, because nobody moved.

One hour later the instructors came wandering out of the office. "Afternoon, girls," one of them greeted us. " Afternoon, Staff," we replied as one.

The pace we were running at was no faster than normal, but I was suffering, I just didn't seem to be able to get the air I required into my lungs. As with the stretcher race, I set myself with false horizons. At the next hill I will stop, I kept telling myself, but on reaching the hill I would continue. The sweat was coming out of me in buckets, I kept seeing bright lights in my vision. Somehow I kept going. At some stage we ended up back at the gym, but I was too far gone to notice. As we stood outside the gym with steam rising off our bodies in the cold air I coughed up some phlegm so I spat it on to the grass. It was a fatal mistake. An instructor walked over, looked at me then walked over to the grass, leant over, and looked at the phlegm I had coughed up. 'Here we go' I thought, 'I am in for a good bollocking.'

"Come here!" he shouted to me.

"Yes Staff," I replied as I ran over.

"Look!" he said pointing to the phlegm. It was dark red.

"Sorry Staff," I said. " Don't be sorry," he said, "it was the blood on your mouth that caught my attention, so go and see the MO".

I tapped on the MOs door.

"Come in!" he shouted. I explained the position to the MO. He examined me, returned to his desk wrote something on a piece of paper, looked up at me and then said, "You're off the course." I was stunned I couldn't believe what I was hearing.

"But, Sir," I protested, "I feel okay." He would not budge. I walked out of his office feeling pissed off and angry. If I had broke my leg, I could have come to terms with it, but a fucking chest infection. I walked over to the Staff instructors office to tell them. The office door was open. Just my luck, they were all piled in there drinking coffee and eating jaffa cakes courtesy of the offenders.

"Aaah, Denmark, we were just talking about you," said one of the instructors as he looked up and saw me in the doorway.

"Was it anything good, Staff?" I asked.

"Yes, it was in actual fact. You are doing well." This made

the pill even harder to swallow. I explained to them what the doctor had said. I suppose I vainly hoped they would have some influence on him, to make him change his mind but it was not to be. They offered their sympathy and told me to give it another go. I was told to clear my bed space and report back to 7 R.H.A. down the road. It was my turn to be cleared out so I didn't rub off on the rest. Because I was a failure. It made no difference that it was not my fault. I packed my kit and made my way down the road. I never saw Clarkey or the rest again, but I like to think they passed.

The following morning I reported to the Air Adjutant for a pep talk. Basically it was his job to try and persuade me to give it another go, but only because the Para instructors had recommended me. He was very nice about it, and pointed out that I had come this far so why throw it all away now.

"You have got the potential to make a Paratrooper," he said "so stay and give it a go."

"Sir, I would like to go back to my regiment in Germany and think about it for a while," I told him. "If you go back there you will never return," he said. I could not face doing it all over again, so that was that it. It was a decision I shall always regret.

I learnt a bit about the Paras during my brief spell with them. It goes without saying that they are hard and tough, but it's not just for the sake of it, they have to be. The Falklands war has shown us that they know how to get that extra mile out of a man when he thinks he can't go on. P Company is hard, but it gets rid of the dead wood, sadly myself included. I challenge anybody who has slagged the Paras off to go and complete P Company and then see if they feel the same.

After a week's leave I made my way back to Germany. As the cross channel ferry made its way into the port of Zeebrugge, I spotted the ill-fated Spirit of Free Enterprise lying on it's side. A shiver ran down my spine as I had sailed

on it many times. I was in a reflective mood as I drove back
to 12 Regiment. I knew I would get a slagging off for failing.
This would come off the tossers who were too scared to have
a go themselves, but I was happy that I would see my old
mates again, especially Mac and Mick.

I arrived at 12 regiment around midday and made my way
to the Battery offices. I was greeted back by the lads after
telling them why I had failed. I caught up on the gossip and
goings on of the regiment. We had a new battery commander
Major, Westlake-Toms. As well as being a dead ringer for
John Pertwee the Doctor Who actor, by all accounts he was
a complete waste of time and morale had hit rock bottom
accordingly. I was summoned to his office for an interview.

"Aach, Denmark," he said looking at the lowly Gunner
before him. "So you failed. Never mind, there's plenty of
hard work for you to do here, so I hope you have some energy
left after all that charging around Aldershot," he said smiling
at his own joke. I made my way back to the accommodation
block.

"So what the fuck am I going to do now?" I thought. Then
I bumped into Mac.

"Scouse, you tosser," he said, "how's it going?"

"Pretty shit mate, as you can see I failed. How about you?"

"I am still doing Northern Ireland training," he said, "and
it's fucking brilliant. By the way," he added, "did you know
22 regiment are going on a Northern Ireland tour." I couldn't
believe my luck. 22 Air Defence were our sister Regiment,
who were located on the other side of the barracks. "When
do they start training Mac?" I asked. "I'm not sure," he
replied, "but it's soon." This was the lifeline I needed, all I
had to do was persuade our battery commander to let me go,
and approach 22 regiment to see if they would take me.

10

The following day I put my plan into action. I decided to go and see the Battery commander of 35 Battery. The reason I had chosen 35 Battery is I had heard that they were under-manned, thus giving me a better chance. 22 Air Defence Regiment was primarily Welsh and I had not had much to do with them, so I wasn't at all sure how I would be received. The first person I bumped into was the Battery Sergeant Major, BSM 'Baz' Guest, and I explained to him about my wish to go to Ireland and basically asked if there was any chance I could accompany 35 Battery. Baz Guest turned out not only to be helpful, he was also a decent man and I liked him on the spot.

"Wait here, young man," he said "I will have a word with the battery commander." And so he disappeared into his office, which had a door connected to the BCs. I kept thinking that the BC was going to come storming out of his office and give me a severe bollocking for taking it upon myself to approach him. The BSM reappeared.

"Young man, the BC wants to see you." I marched in halted and saluted. The BC, Major Hamilton eyed me up and down.

"Stand at ease," he ordered. "My BSM tells me you are very keen to join us for our tour of Northern Ireland," he said, "and why is that?"

"Things are rather quiet at the moment, Sir, and I would love the chance to do some real soldiering, although it may sound corny, Sir, I have wanted to serve in Ireland since I joined the army." Major Hamilton smiled, not even his big droopy moustache could hide it.

"Okay, you're on."

"Thanks sir," I beamed, "I promise I won't let you down."

"One thing," Major Hamilton added, "have you sorted this out with your own Battery?" There was no point in my lying. If found out it would ruin my chances.

"Well, Sir, not really I was going to see my troop commander just as soon as I left here."

"What's your troop commander's name?" he asked.

"Lieutenant Steele, Sir." I replied.

"Okay," he said, "you make your way back to see him and I will speak to him now." I saluted, about turned, marched out and started to make my way across the barracks back to T Battery. I was now very concerned that I had pushed my luck too far, because the first thing my own troop commander was going to hear about this Northern Ireland tour was when a BC from another Regiment rang up to say I would be going. I walked into my Battery offices and tapped on his door.

"Come in," he called. I walked in and saluted Lieutenant Steele. "Are your ears burning?" he asked.

"No, Sir," I replied, "but I think they're about to."

"So you want to piss off to Ireland with 35 Battery, do you?" he said.

"Yes Sir," I replied.

"Okay, then you will be joined by Lance Bombardier Halford, Gunner Poole and Gunner King."

"Okay Sir, that's fine. Thanks." My plan had worked and I was chuffed.

I knew the other lads. They were in my battery so I went to find them and see what they knew. I found John King first. He told me they had got their names down as soon as they

NOT FOR QUEEN AND COUNTRY

had found out about the tour and we would commence
training in two weeks time. I liked John King, he was a
straight-talking lad and Poole, or Skid, as he was affection-
ately known (due to the way he braked when driving) was
also a decent lad, but I was rather more cautious with Andy
Halford, whose nickname was Bags for reasons unknown to
me. I had heard a few unpleasant stories about him dropping
people in the shit for his own ends and given what we were
about to embark on it worried me a bit. I would get to know
John, Skid and Bags well over the coming year.

I was strolling back towards the battery offices when I was
approached by a sergeant who was in charge of the cross-
country team of which I was a member. He asked me if I
was interested in taking part in the Danish marathon in
Copenhagen with the rest of the cross-country team, in order
to raise money for Children in Need.

"When is it, Trev?" I asked, "because I'll probably be in
Ireland a week on Saturday."

"Scouse, you are fucking joking," he said smiling, "you're
fit enough to do it. Come on, think of those poor kids and
the beer after." The beer was the deciding factor "Okay,
Trev, I'll do it," I said.

For the rest of the following week I made the effort to
complete a few long distant runs, though none of them were
anywhere near the 26 miles I would have to do in the Danish
marathon. On the Friday morning before we were due to set
off for Copenhagen. I went up to the bank and changed £200
for Danish Krona using the last of my money before pay day
the following week.

I was sitting in my room finishing the last of my packing
before joining the mini bus outside when I decided to use the
toilet. As I returned from the toilet I caught sight of a member
of the troop leaving the block. He was one of two brothers
in the troop who I shall name Sean and Ian. Sean was a good
lad, but this one who was just learning was a slimy perpetual

thief, he was also as quick as lightning. Then it hit me like a ton of bricks. My wallet! I had in a moment of thoughtlessness left my wallet on my bedside locker. I ran vainly to my room and my wallet was still there, but empty. He had struck again and this time I was his prey. I was gutted. A member of our team kindly lent me some money to see me through to pay day. It was pointless reporting it as I had no proof and the thief was a bombardier who would have given me a hard time. As far as I know he is still at it, but should I ever meet up with him I will show him the error of his ways. The marathon was a success and we raised a decent amount of money for Children in Need.

Skid, John, Bags and me reported to 35 Battery to start Northern Ireland training. We were formally welcomed by the BSM. "Welcome to 35 Madras Battery", he said and then gave us a warning to stay out of trouble whilst attached. The battery would be broken down into troops, the BSM explained. battery headquarters (BHQ), and Seven, Eight and Nine Troops. We were joining 8 Troop under the command of Lieutenant Lovejoy and Staff Sergeant Parsons. There would be around 30 men to each troop we also had a number of REME personnel in our troop.

Each team was made up of four men so Bags, John, Skid and me were a complete team. Bags was the Team Commander, but as we were to find out, more often than not we would patrol with another team, thus becoming a multiple patrol. The BSM gave us a brief outline as to where we would deploy in Ireland. The Battery as a whole would be based in the County Tyrone area but 8 Troop would be based in Strabane, a very nationalist town that lies on the border with the Republic. This would be known as our TAOR, ie, the town and housing estates and rural surrounding, mountains, hills and bogs.

After we had completed two days range practice we would come under the NITAT team. They are a very professional body of men who would teach us every thing we needed to know about Northern Ireland and the terrorist organisations that operate there.

We paraded outside the Armoury ready to get on the wagons that would take us to the ranges. Lieutenant Lovejoy and Staff Sergeant Parsons came over and introduced themselves to our team. I liked them both on sight. Staff Parsons (or Mick as we were ordered to call him, as soldiers don't use rank or surname in Ireland for security reasons) had a look of Neil Kinnock and Lieutenant Lovejoy, or Trev, looked every inch the officer with public school accent. I felt we were in good company.

The whole day was spent shooting. It was boiling hot, but we never stopped for a minute. It was practice I needed. After the second day on the ranges I felt confident that should the need arise, I would be able to hit anything.

The rest of the week we were briefed in detail about the area we were going to and about the terrorists who operated there. I found it fascinating. This to me was real soldiering.

The pace of the training stepped up after the first week. Because infantry work was not our trade as such, we started from scratch. We learned about the unique skills required to patrol in Ireland, and the Army being quick to learn from its mistakes, we had lectures on real events that had occurred, more often than not resulting in the deaths of soldiers and policemen. I was astounded at the amount of weaponry the IRA had in their hands. After most lectures I was left with the feeling that should the IRA want to kill us they would at their choosing, but we would try and make it difficult for them. The IRA also had some very sophisticated explosive devices and we in turn had a range of electronic counter measures, but they were by no means fool-proof.

The NITAT team left us in no doubt that Strabane was considered by all who had served there to be one bad-arse town.

'Bags' began to prove my fears correct within a few weeks. Whenever there was any hard work to be done he would play up on an old army injury he had suffered, a dislocation of some sort. After one such bout of his crying off John remarked what a skiving bastard he was. Bags then began to call John a big nosed twat and it turned into a slanging match and I sided with John, because he was right. It all ended as quickly as it had started, but Bags was left in no doubt as to what we thought of him.

Our team callsign '24A' would often be joined with callsign '23A' as a multiple patrol. 23A was commanded by a REME Corporal called Clegg. His nickname was Boots (due to the fact he did not bull them). The other members of 23A were Miles Milo Gregory (Dunc) who was also a REME full screw and a REME Lance Corporal Smith (Smudge). All the REME lads were technicians by trade so they were very clever, but they were too laid back for my liking. The only exception in their team was Milo who was a Gunner, but as he said very little it was hard to get a feel of his character, but he seemed okay.

We hardly had time to draw breath such was the intensity of the training. The NITAT team proved to be very good at their jobs, using soldiers from other regiments to act as terrorists. The NITAT would send them out into the country-side to test us. These guys would create all kinds of scenarios for us to walk into. At first the situations were obvious, we would find a device sitting next to a hedgerow and the only things missing were the words bomb written on the side. We would all laugh at their attempts to fool us, until, that is, they pointed out a rifle we had strolled past a bit further back. We were still wet behind the ears and NITAT knew this. As time went by however they began to make their mock devices harder to find and so we would look that bit harder. I stopped seeing the countryside for what it was and instead I would look at the hedgerows as hiding places for explosive devices.

Gates were possible booby traps, any rise in the ground could be an IRA gun position. We were no longer casual observers on a Sunday stroll. We searched the surrounding area with our eyes for anything that may indicate danger.

Although we were still in Germany and the terrorists were really soldiers play acting, it felt real. We had to believe in it because our lives would depend on it once we got to Northern Ireland. I enjoyed the lectures that NITAT gave us, they were never boring. They would give us an insight in to the mind of the IRA and how the terrorists operated as individuals and as a cell. We learned how to search people and cars, lorries and buses. Searching vehicles was by far the most difficult. After searching a car for the best part of an hour and finding nothing, NITAT would step forward and pull out a round from some crevice in the car. It was disappointing, but we learned. Days and nights would be spent manning covert observation points (OP). For many tedious hours we would see nothing but once again we learned to be patient despite the cold and tiredness. If we caught one terrorist then all the days of discomfort would be worth it.

Towards the latter stage of our training we moved into a town, purpose built by the Army called Tin City. Tin City mirrored a typical housing estate of the type we would patrol, and once again soldiers on loan from other regiments acted as the hostile inhabitants. A large majority of these men had served in Northern Ireland themselves, so they knew what degree of trouble to give us.

The one drawback with Tin City as far as we the soldiers were concerned, was that everything we did, mistakes and all would be captured on video and played back to a packed hall each morning. The aim of this was not to ridicule anyone, but to once again learn by our mistakes. Far better to make mistakes now while we could all laugh about it, because the IRA would be less forgiving. I began to respect the very cunning ways the IRA operated, they would use all kinds of ingenious ways to reach their target. But the more I learned about them as people the more I loathed their double standards. These so called heroes who were supposed to be fighting the British for their island, would happily stand in the dole offices waiting for their free handouts. As far as they were concerned the British were scum, but a blind eye was turned when it came to dole day.

John, Skid and me had grown very close over the months of training. I could not have asked for two better soldiers to watch my back, but Bags continued to give me cause for concern. He was lazy and he would slope off and skive at any opportunity. Our joint patrol 23A were also knitting together. Boots was still too laid back for my liking as were Dunky and Smudge, but being REME it was to be expected. The only one I wasn't sure of in 23A was Milo but he did seem okay.

The culmination of the Northern Ireland training was a huge riot in Tin City. Our acting terrorists were on top form. As they formed into a mob we came out of our base in full riot gear carrying our riot shields and formed a base line. Within a few moments the mob began to throw lumps of coal which the NITAT team had kindly had delivered that day. We stood firm behind our riot shields, the coal having little effect as it bounced off the shields. One of the NITAT stepped out of the crowd and lobbed a well aimed petrol bomb. It landed just short of our shields and the flames were licking at our boots. "Stand firm", came an order from the rear but the petrol bomb had had the desired effect the mob went wild and began to surge forward. We stood firm and they stopped their advance, but a few of the more daring ones ran at the shields wielding large sticks. They were seized by our snatch squads and dragged by the scruff of their necks behind the base line. The riot began to reach its conclusion and then the whistle blew and it was over. It had lasted no more than thirty minutes but it had felt much longer.

We boarded the wagons and headed back to our barracks in Dortmund. I looked over at John and Skid. They looked like miners just returning from the coal face, as did we all with our faces streaked in sweat and coal dust. Over the past months we had been in a perpetual state of tiredness. I felt exhausted and looking round me I could see everyone felt the same. I was just starting to relax in the comfort that the training was now over, when it struck me that we would be in Northern Ireland for real within a week. So caught up in the training had I become that I had lost sight of the real objective.

We were given a few days off to relax before the move over to Ireland. I found it impossible to relax, though not because of fear. A few weeks earlier I had been patrolling round the barracks and I had taken cover behind a wall in a squatting position, when there was a sudden simulated terrorist attack. I found the squatting position painful at the best of times, but as I sprang to my feet and ran in the direction of the attack I felt the most horrendous pain in my knees. It stopped me dead in my tracks. I had reported sick and the medical officer (MO) had ordered rest and a dose of anti-inflammatory pills. I had been taking the pills, but rest was out of the question and the pain had subsided a touch. I was in something of a dilemma, whether I was more aware of the pain because I had had time to rest for the first time in months I wasn't sure, but one thing I was sure of if I chose to report sick a few days before the Ireland tour and I was kept back people would draw their own conclusions. In other words they may think I was a coward. I chose to say nothing, the MO had already examined me and he was of the opinion that I had strained my knees and that it would eventually clear up. I prayed to God he was right.

11

On Saturday 26th September 1987 we boarded a plane for
Northern Ireland at RAF Gutersloh in Germany. Everybody
seemed to be in a chatty mood and some of the older men
told us about past tours they had been on, days when I was
still at school. Even they had to admit that the training had
changed completely. The terrorists had moved with the times
and so had the army. After a short flight we arrived at Belfast
airport and some of the lads were taken to Strabane in
CPV vehicles. These CPV s were meant to blend in with
normal cars and vans, but it was never long before the IRA
sussed them out so they would have to be changed. The
rest of us boarded a Chinook and as we flew low over the
countryside it all looked so peaceful and normal. We all
looked out of the windows of the helicopter seeing this place
we had heard so much about over the previous months. I
don't know what I had expected but it wasn't this. John turned
to me.

"Scouse, I thought we would be flying into a war zone, not
this," he said.

"I know," I agreed, "it looks so tranquil." The helicopter
settled down in a field at the back of the base and we began
to spill out. Even before we had cleared the helicopter the
soldiers from the Kings Regiment, who we were replacing
were trying to get up the rear ramp in to the helicopter.

"Give them a chance to get off!" barked one of the officers from the Kings. I looked at John.

"Fuck me! Is it that bad?"

"It's not a good sign," John replied with a grin. After much unloading of our equipment and stores the Kingsmen embarked on the Chinook, the huge beast clattered into the air, swung low and it was gone.

We all gathered in to a large hall for a pep talk by the local Royal Ulster Constabulary (RUC). Although we had learned of the area in training, we would now get a real picture of what it was like. The base we would live in lay on the border, it also operated as a checkpoint to monitor traffic crossing over to the south. The river Mourne ran alongside us, we had a small town centre and two very nationalist housing estates: the Ballycolman and the Head of Town. "These estates are very bad," warned the RUC officer, "at the very least you will come under attack from the local youths throwing bricks and petrol bombs. And," he added, "the only way on to the Ballycolman estate apart from helicopter is to cross a bridge over the river Mourne."

The local terrorists were fully aware of this and so the bridge was a perfect place for them to launch a sniper attack. Thus the quicker we crossed the bridge the better, or as practised by the Kings, mingle with the locals as they crossed. It would take a very brave or stupid sniper to risk killing one of their own. The RUC officer concluded his talk by saying, "Forget all the mad dog shit you have been taught it's a different ballgame here."

I was astounded by his last words did he really mean all the training we had undergone was bullshit?

After the talk we were taken to our accommodation. This was an old dance hall complete with reflective balls hanging from the ceiling, with as many bunkbeds squeezed in as possible. It was so cramped that it was impossible to move without treading on someone's kit. I was amazed at how they could fit so many men in to such a small space.

We had just dumped our kit down on our beds when we were told to go and get our flak jackets and helmet visors as we would be going out on our first foot patrol within the hour. John carried a baton gun which fired a six inch cylindrical plastic bullet that could knock a door off its hinges. The purpose of the baton gun was to discourage the local youths from coming too close whilst throwing their bricks at us. Giving them the good news with our rifles was out of the question, no matter how tempting. I was to carry an electronic device that could detect bombs within a certain perimeter of our patrol. It had an ear piece and looked more like a radio but all the locals knew what it was. If I was unlucky enough to hear a certain tone in the ear piece then there would possibly be an explosive device in the area and we would fuck off in the opposite direction fast. The only draw back for me wearing this device was I could not crouch down and take cover behind garden walls and such like because it would affect the range, so out of our patrol I was a good target for a possible shot from a sniper.

Skid, Bags, John and me moved to the unloading bay, loaded our rifles and checked each other. It is vitally important in Northern Ireland that soldiers do not lose any kit like water bottles, ammunition pouches or anything else, because if the IRA find it they may booby trap it hoping a soldier will find it, pick it up and bang, he is blown to bits. It's for this reason also that soldiers are not tempted to pick anything up no matter how innocent the object may look. We were all so nervous as we tried to act professional and macho checking each other. In reality we were green rookies of the highest order and the sad thing is, the IRA are fully aware that the regiments are changing over and the new boys are not familiar with the ground and so often as seen in the past, this is when they attack.

The sentry pulled back the bolt on the huge iron gate. It

swung open a few feet and we darted out. My heart was pounding so hard I thought it was going to come out of my chest. Once we had cleared the base, which is a vulnerable time, we began to walk. I kept expecting to hear the crack of a weapon being fired at us, every car we passed contained a huge bomb in my mind.

I glanced over at Skid, he smiled back. I looked back to check John.

"What's up?" he shouted.

"Nothing," I replied. We were all too anxious for our own good. Bags, who was at the front of the patrol, kept checking over his shoulder to make sure we were still there and I didn't blame him, because the thought of finding yourself alone in amongst these hostile people was too horrible to dwell on. As we made our way along the street towards the town centre of Strabane the thought occurred to me that there were only four of us and thousands of them, although this was by all accounts okay in the town centre, but when venturing onto any of the hard council estates such as the Ballycolman or Head Of Town we would do so in a multiple of no less than eight soldiers. As we moved through the shopping area I looked in to the eyes of the women going about their business, but there was no reaction and they did not acknowledge our presence. It felt so strange to be moving from shop doorways and taking cover against any sniper shots while these people carried on with their mundane tasks. I decided it was time to carry out a P check (personnel check), so I moved across the road to the library and stopped a woman who was about to go in. She was so small and quiet looking that I imagined she was the ideal candidate to try my first P check on.

"Excuse me," I said rather timidly, "can you tell me your name?" Her faced creased up and she turned red, "Fuck off, you British bastard!" she yelled.

"I want your name," I spluttered trying to regain my composure.

"You ain't getting my name, you bastard. The only thing you will get is a bullet in the head, so why don't you fuck off," she yelled. She then spun round and marched off into the library. I knew I could not leave it so I followed her into the library.

"If you do not give me your name now," I demanded in a more aggressive tone," I will have the police out here now." She reeled something off in her thick Irish dialect that was impossible to understand.

"Spell it!" I demanded.

"You thick, British bastard!" she yelled.

"If you could speak the Queen's English, I could understand," I said.

"She's not my fucking Queen," she followed. After another ten minutes of rhetoric I left the library with the information I was after, not that the information was important, but I had made a point.

We would not be fobbed off and I had also had a taste of the feeling the locals had of us. We carried on patrolling through the streets till we arrived at the local bank, and sat on the steps were the local layabouts were drinking cans of beer. They looked more like old tramps than young men on the threshold of their lives. Most of their faces were familiar to me because we had photographs of all the local youth. Some of them were suspected of helping out the IRA. Most of it was low key stuff like carrying messages or keeping a watch while the IRA was up to something, but they were up and coming. They sat there laughing and shouting the odd profanity. I moved up the steps right into their crowd and pulled the biggest and most aggressive looking of them to his feet. He began to protest. "Army brutality," he yelled. I searched him and pushed him back to his sitting position. I lent down and put my mouth next to his ear.

"You fuck round with me and you will be eating this rifle butt! Understand?" The point made I walked down the steps and joined the patrol and we moved on. After my first encounter with the woman at the library I realised that politeness was not the way ahead in Northern Ireland. Bags suggested we go and introduce ourselves at the RUC Station on the edge of town and get a brew while we were there. The RUC Station was no more than a mile from our base, it was a path I would get to know well.

The sight of the RUC Station in Strabane brought home the situation in Northern Ireland. The only resemblance it had to a mainland police station was the illuminated police sign outside, otherwise it looked more like a prisoner of war camp with its armed sentry box and barriers. We unloaded our rifles and joined some policemen in the canteen for a cup of tea. The policemen told us some stories of the Ballycolman estate.

"Youse will get a good bricking on there, so you will," one of them said laughing. "But don't worry," he added, "your first patrol on there will be with us." I was relieved to hear this as I had been told the Ballycolman was a labyrinth of short cuts and alleyways. Having finished our tea we made our way back across town to our base. Anywhere else it would have been a nice fresh September day, but I was sweating buckets because of the bulky body armour we had to wear under our combat jackets. This body armour also had the effect of making us much broader than we were. The locals must have thought we were all bodybuilding fanatics.

On our arrival back at the base we made our way to the collator's office to pass on all the information we had obtained while on patrol. This would include any persons stopped, car registration numbers, sightings of any known IRA members, even down to the fact that the milk was left on the step at a certain house in Railway Street when normally it was always taken in. It builds a picture of the habits of the locals and should those habits change it may indicate that something is about to happen. After every patrol we would go to the collator's office first and spill the beans on what we had seen.

I had just sat down on my bed and was in the process of taking my boots off so I could get a shower when Bags came storming in.

"Scouse," he said, "do you want the good news?"

"Fuck off," I replied, "I'm tired and I am not in the mood. What is it?"

"We're back on patrol in four hours!" I didn't see the point in moaning about it. We had been warned that we would put long hours in. Bags stood there with a grin on his face. "Okay Bags," I said "I heard you. We go back out in four hours."

"There's more," he said.

"Fuck off Bags!" I was starting to get pissed off with him now. "We are going on to the Ballycolman," he bleated like an excited schoolboy.

"It's a wind up," I said.

"It's no wind up, Scouse, we're going on tonight." I trudged over to the shower block in my towel, I felt exhausted. I opened the door to the shower block and stepped in. At first I thought I had gone in to the wrong building or rather a building sight because that is what it resembled. The tiled floor was covered in mud. There stood two rickety shower cubicles one of which had an OUT OF ORDER sign slung across it and, as I was informed by the soldier leaving the other shower, it only ran on boiling hot or ice cold. The two antique washing machines in the corner hadn't fared too well either. There was no excuse for us having to live in these conditions, the job was hard enough.

Besides the cookhouse there was a small cafe run by an Asian man. Most bases in Northern Ireland had them and they were always run by Asians though they are on the decline now as the NAAFI takes over. These cafes are universally known by soldiers as choggie shops, to this day I don't know why they are named as such. Our choggie shop was run by a man nicknamed Smiler. Smiler was a pleasant man and his shop-come-cafe was a small affair consisting of a few chairs, a fruit machine, a counter and Smiler's pride and joy, his sweet display and in the centre of his display was a camera. The camera was nothing special but Smiler had doubled the price on it and when he eventually managed to sell it he would make a killing. In fact Smiler had loaded all his prices, but I suppose he had captive customers. I was to spend many hours in Smiler's shop swigging coffee.

That night as we prepared for our first patrol on the infamous Ballycolman, Bags came out of the OPS room and informed us that the patrol was going to be a mobile with Boot's team and one RUC Landrover. The RUC were really coming along to show us the ground till we were familiar with it. John was in the driving seat, Bags would man the radio in the passenger seat and me and Skid would provide top cover. This involved us standing up through a square hatch in the back of the vehicle so only our heads and shoulders were visible. I would cover the rear with my rifle and Skid would face the front and we would both cover the sides. We were warned to put our helmet visors down once we neared the Ballycolman estate.

"Mount!" shouted a voice from the RUC vehicle which was to lead us.

"Have fun boys," remarked a policeman as he passed us. Bags climbed into the front of the Landrover.

"Are you two okay?" he asked.

"Under the circumstances, Bags, yes, we are," I replied.

"It will be a laugh," he shouted.

"Yes, it will for you, Bags," I said, "you have got protective grills over the windows. Our visors would not stop a brick if we were travelling at any speed. All the engines started up and we moved towards the gate. I had the feeling like when you step on to a roller coaster at a fairground, but I expected this ride to be a little more bumpy. As we approached the

Ballycolman I spotted a sign painted on the wall by local youths. It read "British put your visors down now." Skid and I heeded the warning and just as well we did because a split second afterwards a rock came flying through the air and hit the side of the leading RUC vehicle with a thud.

"Fuck! Where did that come from?" Skid cried out.

"Fuck knows," I replied. It was impossible to tell.

"Bang!" half a house brick crashed into the side of our landrover, but this time I spotted them, four youths standing in an alleyway. "There, Skid," I pointed, but they just stood their ground shouting abuse. "Come on ye British bastards ye." John hit the brakes and we made to dismount and go after them but before we cleared the vehicle they were gone into the warrens of the back jiggers.

We had already been told that it was futile to chase these stone throwing yobs. They could knock on any door and say the Brits after them and they would be given refuge until we had gone.

As we drove further in to the Ballycolman, the stone throwing increased and as each missile hit our vehicle Skid and I would duck down instinctively. We must have looked a sight as we bobbed up and down. Every flat surface be it a garage wall or the gable end of a house had a mural painted on to it, most of the murals depicting romantic images of fallen IRA volunteers who had been slain by the occupying enemy, the British Army. All the murals had been painted by very artistically talented hands. From that second I began to realise why the Americans had been hoodwinked by this propaganda, because these murals were not for the benefit of the local people they were there for who ever came on to this housing estate. If it was the British soldiers, it was meant to intimidate us. If there happened to be a visiting American who was sympathetic to the Irish struggle, even better. He or she could take photographs and show the folks back home and next time the collection tin was passed round they might feel obliged to throw a few dollars in. I don't for one second think any American looked too deeply at why there were names of dead IRA terrorists on these walls and how they really met their demise. Had they had done so they would have discovered not a heroic story of an IRA freedom fighter taking on the British invaders single-handed but a story of a murderer on his way to kill one of his own countrymen in front of his wife and children, because in reality that's how the IRA usually operate.

Before I was posted to Northern Ireland I decided to read a little history of it and try to understand why we were going there. I wanted to know more than the present troubles and I wanted to see further back than that period. I read a few books, most of them biased some of them not. I came away with the opinion that the Catholics had not only had a rough deal over the years but I did not blame them for fighting back, they had suffered great prejudice by their Protestant neighbours in everything from housing to jobs. They were brutally put down if they ever tried to redress the balance; who hasn't heard of the infamous Black and Tans? Sadly though, somewhere along the road to their civil rights the good Catholics of Ireland were politically hijacked by men who took it upon themselves to become the representatives of the people. There was no democracy involved and even to this day these wise Catholics of Ireland keep quiet. The ironic thing about the IRA is that they have gone on to commit the very same atrocities they accused the British of.

As we drove off the Ballycolman I heard a whooshing sound followed by a small bang. A split second later the side of the RUC vehicle burst in to flames. "Petrol bomb!" someone shouted rather belatedly. The driver of the RUC vehicle carried on and although the flames were dying down it was smoking as we drove back to base through the town. The locals didn't give it a second glance, it was obviously a common sight. On reaching the base I made my way over to inspect the damage but apart from some scorched paint work there wasn't any. A policeman saw me looking curiously at a sticky glue like substance where the vehicle had been burned. He went on to explain that sometimes the petrol bombers would leave a number of elastic bands to soak in the petrol for a while, this would reduce the bands to a liquid and once ignited the rubber would stick to the unfortunate recipient and the favoured method of delivery was a small Lucozade bottle because they could be thrown from a safe distance. The only real consolation about petrol bombers was that under the rules of engagement by which we were governed we could shoot the offender (with live rounds) if we considered there to be a real danger to life. I would not like to be the soldier who had to prove it to a court of law.

From the beginning people were losing their tempers with each other, so cramped was our accommodation. Because of the rota with which we operated, there would always be soldiers sleeping while others were just going out on patrol and others came in and in all fairness the majority of the lads made the effort to stay as quiet as possible or as quiet as one can be while getting body armour on and checking this and that. But one or two carried on as though they were at a football match. On more than one occasion I saw a soldier awakened from much needed sleep get out of their bed and punch the inconsiderate offender.

The troop commander, Trev Lovejoy, was quite often in the accommodation making enquiries about our welfare. He made the effort to see the men under his charge and I liked him for this because he had his own worries being in charge of the OP's room. He had to monitor all the radio traffic and liaise with the RUC radio operators and in less hectic moments organise the patrol rosters. My initial feelings about Mick Parsons also proved correct. As a Staff Sergeant Mick really didn't need to go out on patrol but he would often join a patrol, giving someone the chance to get some sleep. He was a strict task master and if crossed would give no quarter, but he was a very professional soldier. Though we soldiers were compelled to work any hours of the day, more often than not all of them, it seems the cookhouse did not. After missing a meal because we were on patrol we turned up with our trays to find the shutters down and this ridiculous situation was repeated time and again throughout the tour. We went into Smilers, he was rarely closed. It seemed we hardly had time to take a cold shower clean our weapons change radio batteries and all the other cleaning, of boots and so on, and it was almost time to be on patrol again. Most of the lads would just crash on to their beds still fully clothed.

On one of the two roads that led from our base to the town centre lay a typically small Irish pub. It was small and rather grubby and as far as I could make out it was devoid of any customers save the odd flat cap I could see at the bar. The landlady was an old woman and from the very first time we patrolled past on foot she emerged from the door with a steaming mop bucket of dirty water which she would throw on to the pavement just short of our boots but ensuring some of the contents splashed on to us. Today it was my turn for the mop bucket treatment. After throwing the water and splashing my pants the old woman's face broke into a grin and she spun round and went back inside the pub. I was raging but it was pointless shouting because she had gone and if reported she would claim it was an accident.

"The old cow," John commented, "she needs that bucket putting over her head." I swore I would get revenge and I suddenly realised the opportunity I was looking for was staring me in the face. On one side of the pub was a window and on the inside was a shelf full of ceramic and brass ornaments and snuggled up in the middle was the woman's big ginger tomcat enjoying the last rays of Autumn sunshine. I crept along the window as quietly as possible and out of sight. I could hardly stifle my laughter at the thought of what was about to happen. At the last moment I leapt up and slapped the window with the palm of my hand. The cat not only cleared every ornament from the shelf it gave out a loud piercing scream. We were gone before the ornaments hit the floor. Little did I know at the time, but fate would bring me and the woman's cat together again.

Further along the street from the grubby pub was a taxi office and perched in the window in a chair was yet another old lady, but unlike the tomcat's owner this old woman never said or did anything. She always had knitting in her hand and a cigarette hanging from the corner of her mouth. The old woman's eyes would follow us till we were out of sight and regardless of the time of day she was always there. Most of the lads had their own theories about the old woman, ranging from her being a IRA lookout to an MI5 plant and as time went by the stories of this woman became more elaborate. One of the lads said she was undercover SAS because she had a moustache.

I became the unelected search soldier in our patrol, the one who would stop and search the locals while the other lads gave me cover but even while searching or questioning someone I would use any available cover to protect myself. If for instance I was near a shop doorway I would back myself in and position the person I was questioning in front of me, therefore reducing the target to any possible sniper attacks. My confidence in searching and questioning grew each time I stopped someone. It was always difficult because it was yes and no answers to everything I asked.

"Where have you just come from?" I would ask.

"Down there," would be the reply.

"Where from down there?"

"Me mate's house."

"Where does your friend live?"

"I just told you, down there." Then I would point out to the person concerned that if it was a time-wasting game they wanted to play then I would be happy to keep them there all day and so they would offer the information I was seeking. Whenever I had to stop and search a person I would, to the amusement of my colleagues, give them the benefit of the doubt and try to be polite.

As we patrolled in to the centre of town, John spotted a car belonging to a known terrorist suspect from the area. We were all familiar with this thug's past exploits but this was the first time we had set eyes on him. He was wheelchair-bound having been shot in the spine by his terrorist bosses for creaming off some of the profits of the bank raids he been ordered to carry out, but the astonishing thing is he received substantial compensation from the Criminal Injuries Board and paid his way back into favour with the terrorist God-fathers. Though he could no longer take an active role in any terrorist activities, he was a suspected courier and a complete pain in the arse to the RUC. I moved round to the driver's side of the terrorist's car, who I shall call Sean Cullen. Cullen was sat in the vehicle with his stereo on full volume staring straight ahead trying to ignore me. I tapped on his window. No reaction, so I banged a little harder. He persisted with his little game of trying to ignore me. This was not unexpected as we had been warned about Cullen's behaviour. Skid positioned himself at the front of Cullen's car and John moved to the rear, Bags watched for any trouble while we were occupied.

Realising that he was going nowhere Cullen lowered the window.

"What the fuck do you want?" he spat.

"What's your name?" I asked in a calm tone.

"For fuck's sake!" he raged "All you Brit bastards know my name, because you have my name up at your barracks, so you do . . ."

"Name?" I repeated. Cullen raised the volume on his stereo, completely drowning out any chance my hearing his reply. He then mouthed his name 'Cullen' and lowered the volume. I called Bags over because he had the patrol radio and I explained Cullen's refusal to give me his name. Bags radioed for RUC assistance, but as soon as he had finished Cullen offered me his name, so Bags cancelled the request for the RUC.

At that moment, a large man with a skinhead haircut came strolling out of a Chinese take-away loaded down with food and made his way towards us. This was Cullen's minder come gopher.

"Fuckin leave us alone, you bastards'!" he bellowed. It was a stupid remark to make considering he had just spent a small fortune on Chinese meals that I would make sure were stone cold before they left. The minder moved up very close to me in a vain attempt at intimidation, the only thing separating us were the trays of food. I put my hand on to his shoulder and pushed him back a foot or so. He did not try and come forward again so the point had been made, I was not fearful of him in the least. I then informed the minder that I was going to search him.

"Under what rule?" he asked.

"You mean under what section." I corrected him.

"Yeah, under what section?" he repeated.

"Under S12 of the Prevention of Terrorism Act 1978," I informed him. "So please raise your hands."

"What about me grub?" he asked.

"Well," I said, "unless you have a talent for balancing Chinese meals on your head I suggest you put them on the ground." During the search Cullen continued to protest at their detention. There was no doubt that Cullen was held in high esteem by the local youths because all of them that passed would shout words of encouragement.

"Are you okay, Sean?"

"Is there anything we can do for you, Sean?" He dismissed them all with a wave of his hand. Some twenty minutes later

146

and knowing that the Chinese food would be stone cold I told Cullen and his thug of a minder that they were free to go. Cullen gave me a fixed icy stare and pointed two fingers to his head as though he were holding a pistol and said 'You.' I smiled back at him.

"Not by you though, Cullen. Well, not unless that wheelchair is turbo driven." As I walked away Cullen shouted.

"You're dead you bastard!" It was water off a duck's back, I didn't bother to turn round and acknowledge him.

Some people may judge our treatment of Cullen and his minder as rather harsh and my comments about his wheelchair to be appalling and very unprofessional, but I would say that Cullen wasn't just a thug off the estate who threw the odd rock at us. He was much more involved and I hated him and everything he stood for. I could not bring myself to even try and speak to him nicely: There was little point anyway.

Although we hadn't completed many patrols in Strabane we were starting to get the feel for the activities of the area. We were naturally vigilant. I know for me personally there was never a moment where I let my mind wander and besides I had a duty to my colleagues and this was reciprocated with John, Skid and Bags. However, Bags was still a first class skiver. He was lazy and as the weeks passed we all felt that it would be much better if he moved to another patrol. Though we hadn't actually said anything to him Bags was fully aware of our feelings towards him and still he made no effort to change his attitude. He was forever calling John 'big nose' as we all had done in the past, but he took it too far. I was fed up of hearing it so it can't have been easy for John but lucky enough for Bags, John had the patience of a saint.

One busy mid week morning our patrol was elected to carry out a foot patrol on to the Ballycolman estate. It was normal procedure to patrol the Ballycolman with at least two patrols, a multiple, but because of the timing it was deemed safe for

24A to go alone. We patrolled out of the base along the street running parallel with the river Mourne which was in full flow because of the recent heavy rain. As we neared the bridge that we had to cross to get to the Ballycolman, Bags shouted back his orders that Skid and him would cover while John and I ran across and so we would then cover them as they crossed.

"Bags," I shouted.

"What's up Scouse?" he asked me as I caught up with him.

"Look," I said, "given the time of day and the amount of people crossing, lets just patrol over amongst them and not scurry across like frightened rats." Bags gave what I had said a second's thought and dismissed it as suicidal, so we crossed the bridge like athletes going for the finish line. I couldn't believe we were on the Ballycolman it was so quiet.

"Fuck me, Scouse, this is not right," John said, "where is everyone?" I had seen people going about their business near the bridge but as we moved on to the estate it was empty. No one came out to brick us. I had a very uneasy feeling. I was sure we were being set up for some sort of attack. I looked across at Skid who had a smile on his face.

"You won't be laughing if we get hit," John shouted to him.

"Do you really not know why its so quiet?" Skid asked with a knowing look on his face.

"Enlighten us," I said.

"Well," Skid went on to explain, if we came on to this estate at one o'clock in the morning, what the fuck would happen?"

"We would get bricked to fuck," Bags answered.

"Well, there is your answer," said Skid, "you can't expect them to stay up half the night throwing bricks at the police and us and then be up all day." Skid was right, as the RUC later confirmed, this was how these people lived their lives.

The following day during a very rare moment of relaxation

I was lying on my bed listening to my personal stereo when I felt a tap on the shoulder. Bags was standing there with a smug look on his face. At first I thought I had been dicked for an extra patrol.

"What's up?" I said hesitantly.

"You remember your suggestion yesterday?" he said. I stared at him my mind a complete blank.

"What the fuck are you on about, Bags?" I said.

"Remember you wanted to walk over the bridge on to the Ballycolman estate."

"Oh that," I said remembering "you're not still pissed off with me are you? For fuck's sake, it was just an idea."

"No, Scouse," he replied, "but I just thought that you might be interested to know that the OP's room have been informed that there was a possible shoot planned for the bridge yesterday." My blood ran cold. What a fucking idiot I had been wanting to put our lives at risk because I wanted to show the local scum that we were not scared of them. When Bags had first told me about the possible sniper attack I thought that he may have collaborated with the guys from the OP's room to set me up, but he was telling the truth and to his credit he never mentioned my stupid suggestion again.

12

The lads moved to the side of the road to provide firing cover. We had decided to set up a VCP on a small road on the outskirts of Strabane. I went through the routine of checking the drivers' documents while Bags radioed the vehicles' registration number to the OP's room, and depending on what kind of information was held on the vehicle and its owner, would determine how thoroughly they would be searched. It was pointless to stay in the location for too long because word of VCP's would spread like wildfire and anybody up to no good would simply wait or choose an alternative route.

We were just about to move on and relocate when a car rounded the bend with English registration plates. This was quite rare in Northern Ireland so out of curiosity I decided to stop it. I didn't for one moment suspect that there would be any terrorist on board, the IRA were not that stupid. I raised my arm stopping the car in the regulation manner whilst still holding my rifle in my other hand. Even before I had made my way to the driver his window was down and he was greeting me.

"This is my wife," he said introducing the young woman in the passenger seat, "and these are my children, say hello children", he instructed the two toddlers in the back of the car. "You are doing the right thing fighting for your country," he went on.

"Thanks," I replied a little puzzled at his enthusiasm for us, "but could I see your driving licence please?" He passed me the licence which gave his address as Croydon.

"What are you doing in Northern Ireland?" I asked him.

"Oh we've been to Dublin," he replied, "and thought we would come and see the IRA."

"Well", I replied, "if you see any please let me know." The smile vanished from his face.

"Who are you?" he asked rather nervously. I realised that this man wasn't joking. "Well, who do you think we are?" I asked him.

"The IRA," he said. Despite our English accents this man thought he had been passing the time of day with terrorists and this was the reason he had been falling over himself to be nice to me.

We moved on to have a look around the graveyard on the Head of Town estate. Like the Ballycolman it is normal practice to patrol in a multiple, but as it was early we were prepared to have a go, if we did not meet too much resistance. Buried in this graveyard were a lot of IRA terrorists, among them were a Charles Breslin and a Michael Devine. These terrorists were local boys who had been ambushed in Strabane by the SAS on their way back from a failed attempt to kill some Police Officers. To this day the Tricolour flies on the spot of their deaths. I was hoping, once in the cemetery, we could have a nose around, but as we neared it some local youths began to stone us and their numbers soon swelled. John loaded the baton gun, more as a visual warning to them to keep their distance and we retreated. I couldn't fathom out why they had become so agitated. I mentioned my worries to one of the OP's room staff on our return to base and my answer came back a week or so later. The guy from the OP's room told me that during a routine search of the cemetery some weapons were uncovered.

Our next mobile patrol was with the RUC. We were back on the Head of Town estate. Over the previous days all patrols had reported being bricked, even more so than normal and if this was so we were in for a heavy bricking. It was pitch black as me and Skid climbed through our hatch on the Landrover to provide top cover.

"Don't forget, Skid, if you see anything let me know," I said as we drove out of the base with our RUC escort.

"Same with you, Scouse," Skid replied. I heard John laughing at our nervous chatter. As we neared the Head of Town, Skid and I dropped the visors on our helmets and lowered ourselves even further into the hatch. We followed the RUC vehicle along a road that ran round the estate with a large wooded bank above us. A bottle flew through the air bounced off my helmet and crashed into Skids visor.

"Where the fuck did that come from Skid?" I screamed.

"I don't know!" he yelled back "It's too dark to see." And then all hell let loose. "Bang" Our landrover jumped into the air. A huge stone the size of one of the landrovers wheels crashed on to the bonnet. Sparks flew as the stone tore into the metal and then another huge stone landed on the top of the landrover missing Skid by inches. The fire extinguisher we kept on board in case of petrol bomb attacks flew through the air.

"They're rolling them down the bank at us" Skid yelled out.

"John get the fuck out of here!" I screamed. But John was blocked in by the RUC vehicle which had stopped. If one of the boulders had hit me or Skid we would have been killed just by the sheer weight. In a moment the stones stopped and an angry mob of youths came storming out of a darkened alleyway, pelting us with bricks and bottles. I turned towards the new onslaught of aggression. As the bricks and bottles crashed into our visors and helmets Skid and me both began crying out to John, "Just fucking drive. Now!"

Four or five of the mob ran to the back of our landrover and began punching and clawing at my legs and trying to pull me out. Others were probing in the darkness for anything they could pilfer out of the vehicle. I pulled my boot back and gave a well aimed kick to the nearest face, he let out a scream of pain as my boot made contact and the mob drew back.

Our Landrover began to move off fast. Bags had managed to get through on the radio to the lead RUC vehicle and tell them of the desperate situation we were in. He then radioed the base to tell them that we had lost our fire extinguisher and they promptly ordered us to try and retrieve it! Bags explained that it had been seized by an angry mob and we would be putting ourselves in a very dangerous position if we tried to get it back. The OP's room reluctantly told us to return to base. Only on our return and when they had seen the boulders and damage to the landrover did they apologise for ordering us back into the Head of Town estate.

I learned a lesson about the events of that night and it is that the RUC, who are enclosed in their vehicles and therefore protected from the bricks and bottles don't get a true picture of the severity of some of these brickings the soldiers have to endure, and that is why the RUC vehicle was so slow to move off, whilst we were being attacked.

John, Skid and I spent all our spare waking moments drinking coffee in Smiler's. It was a pleasant place to sit and moan about things and talk about Bags behind his back. On one such day a few of the lads walked in and began to play Smiler's prized fruit machine as they frequently did and as always Smiler watched intently which was a sure sign that the jackpot was about to drop. As Skid, John and I joined them around the machine, one of the lads commented about Smiler watching us.

"Yes," said one of the assembled crowd "and while he is watching us, he has his back to his display of sweets and the jewel in his crown, his beloved camera." With lightening speed a plot was hatched while Smiler looked on totally oblivious to what was going on before him. One of the assembled crowd left our party and made his way around the back of the building outside Smiler's shop. Once there he slid his hand through the small window. For me watching from inside, I could see the hand carefully feeling around the display. We all yelped with mock delight to keep Smiler's attention. The hand located the camera and it disappeared through the tiny window never to be seen again. Once the sneaky plot had taken place we all made our excuses and left. As the last person left I heard Smiler come from behind his counter saying he had to lock up because he needed to go somewhere, but we all knew it was so he could chance his luck on the fruit machine. There was uproar when we returned from patrol with everybody looking for Smiler's camera. It was never found and from then on Smiler eyed us all with suspicion.

It wasn't long before I finally got to have a look around the cemetery on the Head of Town estate. It was part of a joint patrol with the RUC during the dark hours. I had a look at the grave of Charles Breslin out of sheer morbid interest and then I went in search of any more Republican plots whose occupants had been dispatched while trying to murder somebody. It was so dark I gave up and moved back over towards Breslin's grave. I could just make out the shape of an RUC officer rising from a squatting position.

"Have you just had a shit on his grave?" I asked on reaching him.

"Let's put it this way son," he replied, "I have more respect for any shit that maybe lying on that there grave than the shit lying inside it."

We patrolled away from the graveyard and headed off the

estate. Just as we passed the last house, there flattened and nailed to a tree, was the fire extinguisher we had lost a few nights before. There but for the grace of God goes me I thought.

Sitting on my bed one night I was chatting with John when Bags returned from the OP's room where he had gone to get the patrol roster.

"Right, gather round," he said excitedly.

"What's up Bags?" I said surprised to see him so enthusiastic about work.

"Okay", he said going on to explain. "Whenever we go to the Head of Town estate we get bricked!"

"Yes", John interrupted "Now tell us something new for fucks sake."

"Shut the fuck up and let me finish!" Bags shouted angrily at John. "There have been reports that everytime the shit come out and brick us that there have been sightings of a gunman following behind them openly on show. So what the powers above want is for us to stick our necks out a bit and go on to the Head of Town estate and cause a bit of friction. So when the gunman shows the SAS are going to bang him!"

"Kill him," I said fully understanding what Bags had said but wanting to confirm it.

" Yes," he replied, "waste the bastard." Unable to contain my delight at being able to take a small part in the killing of a terrorist, I went on to quiz Bags.

"When is it set for? Who else will take part? What happens after they have shot him?" But Bags could not confirm anything.

"I don't know yet," he said "They will let us know." Unfortunately a few days later the set-up to kill the gunman was cancelled and no reason was given. I was shocked by this planned killing of an IRA gunman, not out of any concern for him because these murdering scum deserve no more, but by the way we had talked of the plan around my bed as though we were talking about something trivial.

October 1987 saw some severe storms lashing the United Kingdom, and Northern Ireland was no exception. For over a week the rain had poured down relentlessly. There was no let up. Each time we went on patrol we could see that the River Mourne had risen. In fact it had risen so much that the only thing holding it back was a drystone wall. Though the river ran parallel to our base we were lucky because it was built on a small hill and it sloped off towards the town centre.

I was in a deep sleep when Skid woke me up.

"Scouse, get dressed, we have got to go out now!" he urged. I glanced at my watch, it was 8 pm and we had only just come off a patrol at 6 pm.

"Skid, if this is a wind up, I'll smack you," I said.

"It's not, Scouse," he pleaded. "The river has burst its banks and the whole town is flooded out," he continued.

"Where's John?" I said still half asleep, then it hit me he wasn't with us. My name had been pulled out of the hat to attend a fancy dress party in Londonderry, a party the RUC had organised. John had begged me for the tickets, so I let him take my place. As I pulled my boots on Mick Parsons came in to the room.

"Get a fucking move on Scouse these people need our help", he said.

"What? You mean the same bastards who are trying to put a bullet into our heads, Mick?" I replied.

"Okay, Scouse, I take the point," he said "but its not my orders".

We moved to the OP's room for a briefing where the troop commander, Trev Lovejoy, gave us our orders.

"Go out and just see what you can do," he said. "Give assistance to the RUC if and when needed and make sure the local shite are not looting."

"What about boats?" some one enquired from the back.

"Boats?" I repeated, "how fucking deep is it?"

"Waist deep and getting deeper," someone answered.

A patrol was making its way back into the base when the dry stone wall exploded under the pressure of water. Faced by a wall of water they turned to run, but it was useless. They were washed halfway back down the street along with parked cars. Miraculously none of the patrol was killed or even injured. One of the patrol told me later that he was more concerned about losing his weapon.

We moved out of the base, down the slope and walked to the water's edge. It was like looking out over a lake, but this lake had houses jutting up above the surface. I could see where cars had been washed along the street as though they were dinky toys. They were piled up in a large heap between two houses taken there by the first gush of water. We waded into the freezing water and began to make our way towards the town centre with the intention of checking on the houses as we did so. To my amazement most of the homes still had electricity. All the occupants had fled to the upstairs and they were yelling out of their windows most asking if it got any worse would we airlift them out? I assured them that they would not be abandoned. It was a very odd situation because these people who hated us were now asking for our help, speaking to us in a polite manner. Because of the situation an unofficial truce had been called.

It was impossible to walk in the centre of the road-river because the current was so fast. We moved along with great care because there was a lot of debris under the water. Despite this I lost my footing and before I could recover the current had me in its grasp. In that moment as I went under the water I realised we had all made a mistake and I was about to pay for it. We had, in our rush to get out put on our body armour. To the casual observer this may sound like madness, but such was our conditioning and routine that it

157

never entered our heads to leave them off, as are the regulations whilst on rural patrols because of the need to cross rivers. As I used the last of my energy to hold on to a street sign a hand gripped the back of my collar and pulled me clear. My rescuer was Brownie, a coloured lad from another team. I couldn't thank him enough but he just laughed it off.

"You would do the same for me," he said and he was right. We would all help each other.

We vowed to ditch the body armour on our next visit to base. Since my knee injury in the Ireland training I had suffered almost constant pain, but now in the freezing water I could feel nothing. Bags quite rightly was concerned that if he was to fall we would lose all communications.

"There are enough RUC in the area, Bags," I assured him, "and if the worse comes to the worse we can return to base." I thought of John who was probably drunk and blissfully unaware of what was happening back here in Strabane.

"Help me! Please help for God's sake!" I moved on further along the street to the source of the shouting. A woman in a near hysterical condition was yelling down from a bedroom window. On seeing me she began shouting.

"Soldier, it's me Mam and Dad, you have got to help them. Please, they are in a bungalow a bit further up the road. Please help them. This will kill them!"

"Okay," I shouted back to her, "I will go and look for them, just calm down, they will be okay." After the woman gave me the number of the bungalow, Skid and I began to wade along the street to where the woman had said her parents would be. It was hazardous because of all the debris rushing past on the strong current. Below the surface I felt a sharp pain as something smashed into my shins, but we had no option, other than to press on. We reached the bungalow and I looked in through the living room window. Amazingly the lights were still on, despite the water inside being waist deep.

"Fuck me, I can't believe the electricity is still on!" Skid said.

"I know," I replied, "but I will have to look for them, they might be in the back somewhere."

"Or worse," Skid said, " they may have tried to get out, and if that's the case they are past our help." I picked up a piece of wood that was floating around in the front garden and smashed the living room window and climbed in. Skid waited outside because even in these desperate circumstances we could not trust the people in case it was a trap. The living room was completely destroyed. Everything was floating or submerged in the filthy cold water. The settee was bobbing around along with photographs, rugs, and clothing. The telly was just visible under the surface of the water. The smell in the house was nauseating, but I just assumed that this was something that the water had flooded in.

"Hello is anybody home? This is the army."

"In here," came a faint reply from the back of the bungalow. I forced open the living room door and waded in to the hallway. The smell of shit was now so overpowering that I nearly threw up and the reason soon became apparent. The force of the water had pushed all the waste from the toilet, and there were huge turds floating on the water and I was standing in it. With a great push I forced the bedroom door open and there was the old man and woman sitting on their overturned wardrobe floating. If it hadn't been in such tragic circumstances I would have laughed, but these people were old, soaking wet, very cold and frightened and no doubt suffering from hypothermia.

"Are you okay?" I stupidly asked.

"I'm tired," the old man replied.

"Well, let's get you out of here then," I said. Between Skid and I we managed to get the old couple out and load them into a boat. I was able to tell the woman that her parents were safe and she couldn't thank me enough, but I was under no illusion that once the water subsided so would the goodwill.

Bags, Skid and I decided to take the offer of a lift on one of the boats back to the base. We needed to rid ourselves of our body armour and get warm because we were now in danger of coming down with hypothermia. We had been in the freezing water for hours and I certainly felt weak. As we made our way back to the base along the street which now resembled a river I took stock of the damage. A mini car floated past us, its wiper blades still in motion, but thankfully it was empty. Broken trees, boxes, furniture, rubbish of every description, floated by on the fast current, even the outboard motor was struggling against the current. The boat scraped the road as we hit the tarmac at the base and splashed the few feet to dry land. Trev Lovejoy the Troop Commander was there to greet us.

"What's it like out there, lads?" he asked us.

"Its fucking awful Sir, there's not much we can do, the water is too deep at the moment."

"Okay," he replied, "go and get warmed up and get some hot scoff and be back here in an hour, your team can go back out with Staff Parsons." I was glad Mick Parsons was coming out with us because he would not take any fucking about from anybody.

"Where the fuck are the boats coming from?" Bags enquired as we made our way to the cookhouse. "I don't know Bags and I don't care," I replied I felt exhausted and I was too cold to give a shit.

We arrived at the cookhouse to find it closed!

"Where the fuck are the cooks?" I asked one of the lads who was walking away looking pissed off.

"They said they won't get up till breakfast," he replied.

"The lazy bastards!" I shouted hoping they could hear me. I looked at my watch, it was only just after two am.

"So much for getting some hot scoff!" Skid said.

"I know," Bags said and he walked over to Smiler's shop and began hammering on the door.

"Smiler, wake up you lazy bastard," he shouted "there's trouble!" Smiler's shop doubled as his bedroom. After a while the door opened and he appeared.

"What you want?" he asked. "It still night time." We explained the devastation outside, of which Smiler was oblivious, but he didn't hesitate to open the shop for us and I felt guilty for laughing about his camera. We sat in Smiler's drinking hot coffee and eating chocolate bars when Mick Parsons came in.

"Cancel your last order, lads," he said, "there is no point in us going out now while its dark, we would just be fucking about for nothing. We will go out at first light."

"At last," I thought, "some common sense."

"By the way Scouse," Mick added, "we have got to go to the other side of town and pick John King up at about 10 this morning."

"Mick," I replied, "do you know he is dressed up as a beach boy?"

"Oh, fucking great!" he said, "that's going to look good if there's any press there." There was a serious side to it because John was in a very vunerable position.

At first light Bags, Skid and me joined Mick Parsons and a policeman as we climbed into the boat. Mick was quick to notice the worried look on our faces.

"Relax lads I'm an expert at boats," he laughed.

"Which sides are port and starboard?" Skid asked

"Fuck knows," Mick replied "as long as I can aim it where I want to go, who gives a shit?"

We set off down the flooded street towards the town. The current hadn't weakened at all. A boat sped past us at full throttle with another team on board and at the helm was a guy from our troop George Harland. George was one of life's rogues he didn't give a shit about anything.

"Morning, ladies", he screamed out laughing as he whizzed past.

"That fucking idiot will come a cropper," Mick Parsons said smirking.

As luck would have it our intended route took us past the pub where the old lady would come out to soak us with her mop bucket full of water. Alas that was out of the question for today at least, and what's more she was in her upstairs window which was not too far above us because of the water level. The old woman was waving frantically trying to attract our attention.

"I suppose we should see if the old bat's okay," Mick said closing down the throttle on the boat's engine. Either by good luck or management Mick guided us right under her window. I stood up to see what the old woman wanted. I tried to communicate to her to lift the window but from what I could make out it was stuck fast. I sat back down.

"What does she want us to do?" the policeman asked.

"Smash her window so she can tell us", I said in a half joke. The policeman promptly stood up removed his pistol from its holster, and smashed the pane of glass with the butt. The old woman began screaming and shouting.

"Ya bastards ye. Why the fuck did ye smash me window? I'll fucking have ye for this!" she shouted at the poor policeman. He turned to me looking for a answer, I just smirked.

"You bastard!" he said "If I get in the shit for this I will have you." After another half hour of pacifying the old woman, the policeman learned she was only looking for her cat.

"If we find it, we"ll bring it back!" Mick shouted to her, as he opened the throttle and we carried on. Thankfully the policeman did see the funny side of my joke, it had been too good an opportunity to miss.

We had gone no more than fifty feet when we heard an almighty grinding noise coming from the propeller.

"Oh fuck," Mick shouted, "look!" And there we saw, was the reason for the noise. Mick had gone over the top of a car, which now had a roof which resembled an opened bean can. Our propeller was also somewhat reduced, but it still worked.

The occupants of the flooded houses seemed resigned to their fate, they just stared at the stupid, cold, and wet soldiers zipping around in boats below them. We headed into the town centre where we had an appointment to pick up the beach boy himself, John King. The plan was that we would go to the nearest dry piece of road and radio the base, tell them of our position and the car would drop John off. That was the plan. On entering the town square, we found that the window of a local supermarket had caved in. Mick skilfully navigated the vessel through the broken window and we began a trolley dash with a difference. The policeman looked away with a grin on his face. Smiler didn't sell one jar of coffee for the rest of the tour! I was to learn later, that some of the lads had emptied a Chelsea Girl shop.

The boat laden with goodies, we sped across the water to the dry part of the town where a crowd was gathered watching the floods. Standing in the middle still in his Beach Boy outfit was John King. Irrespective of how funny it may have looked it was a very dangerous position to be in. Here stood a British soldier, unarmed, surrounded by hostile natives. Why they never kidnapped him, I shall never know, maybe it just never crossed their minds that he was a soldier. It might be that they were so preoccupied with the water that they never noticed. John was a lucky man that he was able to climb into our boat. Just over a year later the World would witness what these barbarians were capable of, when two unfortunate soldiers were captured by a mob after they had strayed into a funeral.

The boat struggled as we fought against the current, which was hardly surprising considering our extra booty. A boat full of policemen passed us.

"Go to the cricket pitch!" one of them shouted across with a smile on his face.

"Why?" I shouted back.

"Because some of your lads have got themselves into a little difficulty," he replied with a grin still on his face.

"That will be fucking George," Mick said, "we had better go and see what the stupid bastard's done." We arrived at the cricket pitch, which now looked more like a boating lake, to find George and his merry band of men standing waist deep in water.

"Where's the fucking boat George?" Mick shouted angrily at him.

"Sorry, boss," George shouted back, "it was an accident. I turned too fast and it just filled up and sank."

"Where the fuck is it?" Mick repeated.

"Here." George said, pulling the submerged hull from the water. George, his men and boat had to be recovered. I slumped in to my bed exhausted when we finally got back. We had worked in the freezing water for hours.

The following day we were able to resume normal patrols on foot! All the flood water had drained away leaving the debris and sludge behind. Most of the homes had been damaged, and sadly not a lot of them had been insured. The secretary for Northern Ireland, Tom King, arrived onto the scene in a show of concern by the Government. He looked round a few of the damaged shop premises, muttered how bloody awful it all was and then he was gone. Public relations exercise over.

Some of the lads were pictured on the front pages of the tabloids, under headlines of 'hero' and such. The only exception was the local IRA rag, which told stories of soldiers looting peoples' houses and watching old people struggling in the waters. What all this bullshit amounted to, was that the IRA were gutted that the Army had had a chance to help the local population and they, the locals, had accepted that help.

Bags, true to form, was taken out of front line patrolling due to some medical problem. I didn't even bother to find out, because I had known it would happen sooner or later. Bags' replacement was an REME fullscrew called Colin Roberts. Colin was a very able and likeable soldier and he fitted in well, so morale in the team picked up following Bags' replacement.

A tragic event occurred while we were out on patrol that was low down, even by IRA standards. It was Remembrance Sunday 1987. We took cover to stop and remember the dead at 11 o'clock, when the radio burst into life with reports of an explosion of some sort. All the lads seethed at the timing of the attack, but it was only when we returned to base that we learned of the full horror of the attack at Enniskillen, just down the road. Words failed me. Unfortunately more tragedy was to follow.

Just before Christmas a multiple patrol had returned to the base and were in the process of being debriefed, when there was a loud and unmistakable sound of a gun being fired. Moments later a policeman came running into the room screaming and totally incoherent. The soldiers went to look for themselves and discovered the body of the policeman's colleague. He had been shot in the head. The rumours were going the rounds within minutes of this tragedy. Some of the lads were saying it had been an accident, others suggested that the policeman had been playing Russian roulette. Whatever, it was a life had been lost and the sadness affected everybody.

We continued to patrol Strabane and the surrounding housing estates with a monotonous regularity. For our troubles we still got a daily dose of bricking and insults. More so on the housing estates, because the town centre was quiet until the IRA made their first move against us. There was a gap between two shops that had been boarded up, hiding the waste ground. The boards had been painted over showing a picture of father Christmas and his reindeer. The children loved it, but the local IRA unit saw it as a wonderful place behind which to hide an explosive device, and then they detonated it as an RUC patrol passed. The policemen took the full force of the blast, but by some miracle none of them were killed, though they did suffer some very serious leg injuries.

Patrolling the town centre on Christmas Eve was an experience for me. I was to see the local thugs at their worst fuelled by beer, which they were drinking in large quantities. They were spoiling for a fight, or aggro of some kind. Our team had been unlucky enough to draw the short straw for mobile patrols. (I suspected it was fixed!) I lost count at the number of beer bottles that were thrown at us. I personally kept my helmet visor up while we were parked in the town centre, hoping to reply in kind with a baton round. John and I were once again providing top cover, and I was facing to the rear of our Landrover. A group of the local scum were passing with their girlfriends and shouting the same old insults. 'British bastards' 'Brit tossers'. It was water off a duck's back, we had heard it all before. Suddenly one of the lads in the group broke away and walked over to me and made as though he were about to throw a bottle of beer he had in his hand. His friends were laughing and daring him to throw it.

"Go on," they encouraged, "hit the Brit bastard in his face. He's ugly already it won't make any difference." At this point I was very tempted to lower the visor on my helmet, but then I thought if I did this, it would be an invitation for him to throw it. He stood there his lips curled in anger uttering obscenities at me. The lads watched to see the outcome of this stand off.

"You, Brit bastard, are getting this bottle in your face!" the lad shouted. I raised the baton gun and said.

"Go on then you thick Irish bog trotter, I dare you to, and when you have I shall fire this baton round into your acne ridden face."

"Go on throw the bottle at him," urged the girls. Without taking my eyes off my aggressor I spoke to the group behind him. "He won't throw it because he is a spineless bastard." He began to shake. "Go on shithouse," I goaded him, "please give me an excuse to alter that sad fucking mess of a face of yours." The lad threw the bottle to the ground and stormed off shouting that I would regret my words.

"Scouse, would you have fired?" Skid asked me later on. "Yes," I replied without hesitation and meant it.

Shortly after Christmas we packed our kit and moved by helicopter to another border town called Castlederg. From here we would begin the rural phase of our Northern Ireland tour. We would patrol the surrounding countryside and the nearby Sperrin mountains. This was a different ball game altogether. We would use very different patrolling techniques. Off went the body armour and on went the Bergen. We would no longer have the luxury of being able to call in at the base or RUC for coffee and a rest, now we would be negotiating rivers, fences and ditches, and patrols would extend for days rather than hours, and to add to the misery the weather had turned very cold.

13

I had already been warned that the accommodation in Castlederg was in a chronic state of disrepair, and I wasn't disappointed. Boot's team, 23A, and our team were bunked together in an old Portacabin, which had a hole down one end with a bucket below it to catch the rain. The showers worked but only sometimes.

From this point in the tour, we would operate as a multiple patrol with Boots' team. From a security point it was considered better to patrol the countryside with eight men as opposed to four and this did make sense because if the IRA did decide to take us on in a fight, they would be in large numbers.

It pains me to admit that we were not very well prepared for the conditions that we would be patrolling, despite our training, but we were about to learn fast. Our first patrol in to the cold and wet border was at midnight. We would be dropped at a point by the helicopter and follow a route back to the base, searching farmhouses and looking for men wearing balaclavas and carrying guns on the way! I packed my Bergen with a sleeping bag, in case of a casualty, spare clothing, a flask and one or two other essential items. John carried a nightsight on his weapon and I had a telescopic sight. The sight had a trilux pointer which illuminated at night, so it was easier to get a good aim on a target. All the boys were slapping a waterproofing dubbing over their boots. I didn't need it because I had invested in a pair of gore-tex boot liners, but even these would prove to be useless after our first river crossing.

I had a spare half hour before the patrol so I walked across to the cookhouse for a brew. As I was walking back I was stopped by an officer. This particular officer had not been out on patrol since we arrived, he had in fact had a desk job, but no one could work out what it was. He flicked his well groomed hair back, which was well over the regulation length, and said

"Where are you going?"

"Back to the Portacabin," I replied.

"After that?" he asked. I checked my watch.

"Well, out on patrol in ten minutes Sir," I said.

"Why are you dressed like that?" he then asked. It was raining hard by now and time was running out.

"Sir with all due respects," I said, "what is the point to all this, only I am due out on patrol very soon?"

"Yes," he replied, in a much more hostile tone, "there is a point to all this. You cannot go out on patrol in those waterproofs."

"Sir," I protested, "it's lashing down with rain and very cold."

"You know what the NITAT team told us." he went on, "These waterproofs make too much noise."

"Yes sir," I agreed, "but the NITAT team told us a lot of things that don't apply in the real world of Northern Ireland."

"That may be so," he said "but tell the rest of your team, no waterproofs." With this he walked off back to his plush accommodation, no doubt to sit and watch telly. Another fraud who would pick up a medal. I told Boots, who was the most senior rank in the multiple, what the officer had said.

"Okay." he replied, "we shall have to bin the waterproofs."

I half expected Boots to obey the officers order, even though it was absurd, because although Boots thought he was a good soldier, he was rather timid in the face of any confrontation.

As we stood in the pouring rain on the perimeter of the base the helicopter swooped out of the inky black clouds. The pilot gave us the thumbs up and we ran forward to the Lynx, stowed our Bergens on board and climbed in. The machine hovered, the nose tilted and we were away. The only thing visible to me was the lights from remote farmhouses below. The pilot wore passive night goggles. The night vision aid turned night in to day. In the warmth of the helicopter I felt safe and sleepy. I felt like nodding off as it pitched and turned. Boots had passed our co-ordinates to the navigator and we had faith in these flyers because if it was the corner of a desolate field we wanted to go to then that's where we would go. All too soon I felt the familiar judder as the helicopter lost altitude.

It touched down, the doors slid open and we went through a well rehearsed drill of all around defence, but this time it was for real. In the best traditions of the Army Air Corps they dropped the soldiers and hightailed it out of there. We lay still for a moment. The only noise was the wind and the rain beating against my face.

"Has everyone got their rucksacks?" Boots whispered

"Yes," came the reply from everyone except Duncan Gregory. Boots asked him again

"Duncan, have you got everything?"

"Yes," he said.

"Well then, fucking answer me then," Boots shouted. I liked Duncan, he was laid back in the REME fashion and would not speak unless he considered it to be important, a habit that irritated a few of the lads who could not work him out.

Boots consulted the map one more time and we set off for a farmhouse a mere two miles away. There was no comparison to the urban patrolling we were used to, this was a different world. We had covered a little distance before we encountered a barbed wire fence. I could hear swearing as clothing was ripped and flesh was torn. Bergens were taken off, heaved over then put back on. It was stupid and impossible to climb over still wearing them. A hundred feet further on, across our path, we found a huge water-filled ditch with sharp spiked brambles on each bank. Our efforts to cross it without a complete soaking were in vain, not that it made much difference because the rain had not let up for a second. I had to laugh at the lads' efforts to keep their feet dry with the dubbing on their boots. It had been completely washed off. My gore-tex socks were now full of water and the only way to empty them would be to take my boots off.

We arrived at an old barn next to a farmhouse, but not the farmhouse we had been tasked to search, we were still over a mile from that.

"What the fuck are we going to do?" I asked Boots.

"We will have to carry on," Boots replied.

"You are fucking joking?" someone said.

"We are all soaked to the fucking skin," John shouted, "some cunt will come down with hypothermia." John was right, though I had kept it to myself I was starting to feel the effects of the cold. I had said nothing because of the slagging I might get.

"Look, Boots," I said, "I don't give a fuck what that bastard officer says I am wearing my waterproofs on the next patrol."

"So am I," he replied. After ten minutes of shivering we decided to head for an RUC station which was half a mile away. Against all the rules we had been taught we crossed bridges, walked through gates and we arrived in less than half an hour. Against Boots' better judgement we stayed there for most of the night.

On that first patrol we all learned many valuable lessons. The tasks we were given were impossible to achieve, unless, we took short cuts. Some people may look on it as cheating, but whatever it was, it was necessary. If there was a bridge over a river, we felt that it was worth the gamble of crossing, to stay dry. If there was a gate we ran through it, rather than spending time crossing barbed wire fences. Even in this blatant disregard of the rules we tried to make it hard for any potential bomber, by running through the gate one at a time so if the worst did happen they would only get one of us. But often there was no short cut, so we would have to climb the fence anyway. After only a few patrols we began to get more competent. Instead of trudging along wet and miserable, we were staying dry and therefore able to concentrate on the most important reason for our presence, catching the terrorists at it, and restricting their movements.

The base at Castlederg was worse than Strabane, if that's possible, we didn't even have the luxury of Smiler's shop. Patrolling in rural areas was much harder mentally, because we always had to be aware that we no longer had the protection of people who were around us in Strabane. Here we were isolated so any device the IRA detonated would not hit any innocents. In actual fact we were sitting ducks. We would spend hours patrolling along side roads looking for any wires that may possibly be attached to a device. Rightly or wrongly we had little faith that we would ever find any wires, the IRA were not that dumb.

It did not take us long to visit our first 'tea shop'. Mr and Mrs O, as I shall call them, had a son who was a member of the RUC so we knew she was okay. It would have been foolhardy to just bang on Mrs O's door and ask for a brew. We had been tipped off how to go about it. One of the team would knock on Mrs O's door and ask if we could search her barn. If she had company or if she felt it was unsafe she would say yes go ahead. If however the coast was clear she would invite the soldier in and then his colleagues would emerge from the bushes, as we did this day.

"Go in there boys," she said as we all trooped into her living room. "Sit ya selves down," she urged, "I will fetch youse some tea."

We all sat down on the sofa. The log fire was blazing away, the telly was turned on and ten minutes later Mrs O appeared with eight mugs of steaming tea and a tray of cakes. Boots began to look a little uneasy.

"Mrs O," he said, "we can't possibly let you go on buying us all these cakes."

"No," she replied, "my husband delivers coal and all the shops hand them over for free."

"Oh if that's the case," Boots said helping himself to a cake.

During the hour or so we were at Mrs O's we learned that she had a daughter who also provided tea and cakes.

"Does her husband not mind?" someone asked probing.

"Oh no," Mrs O. replied in all innocence, "she's not married." Eight pairs of ears pricked up at this information. Mrs O's daughter, Tracy, would be getting a visit. Though we felt rather guilty sitting in Mrs O's house drinking tea and eating cakes when we should have been patrolling, once inside the door the guilt would evaporate and our hourly visits began to stretch to two or three hours. If we arrived at Mrs O's and she had visitors we would all walk away feeling pissed off.

"Never mind we will have to go and patrol," Boots would say. Unfortunately Mrs O's daughter lived some distance away from her, so it was not possible to slip from one to the other. It depended what patrol route we had been given as to who we would visit. As for Mrs O's we would all hide while Boots went into his routine, but Tracy never turned us away. The only drawback with her house was that sometimes we would arrive to find another patrol had beaten us to it. Tracy had a mate Anne and both of them were getting a seeing to by the lads from another team. Anne had teeth a racehorse would have been proud of, but as the lad who was seeing her put it, any port in a storm.

When not skiving in Mrs O's or her daughter Tracy's we did try and complete the tasks we were given. The weather had turned very cold by now, so we often made use of a barn to shelter in and have our scoff, and then we would move on. We were fully aware that it was dangerous to use the barns, and so we took turns to stand outside and keep a watch and this day was no exception. Boots called Skid into the barn from outside where he had been watching.

"Right, get your shit together!" Boots shouted, "we are moving out of here." Boots and his team moved out of the barn, while we waited to give them some distance before we would also move out. But this time they had gone only a short distance when all hell let loose.

I could hear shouts of "Contact". The word 'contact' means there has been some form of attack. Then I heard the sound of distant gunfire. All of our team legged it from the barn across the road and took cover behind a bank where Boots and his team were laid up.

I turned to Colin who was taking cover next to me. "You're the fucking commander, get a grip and find out what's going on."

The situation was ridiculous. All the lads were shouting about what they had seen. I personally hadn't seen anything at this stage and for all I knew the shots had come from behind me. Boots crawled over and slid in between me and Colin. He pointed to a small hill in the distance. Trying to catch his breath, he went on to explain that two men dressed in what he thought were combat jackets and carrying rifles had fired towards him.

"Are you sure they're not soldiers?" I asked Boots.

"No, they had fucking jeans on," he replied, "I know they are not fucking soldiers."

"Well have you radioed a contact?" I asked him.

"Yes, of course, I fucking have!" Boots shouted back. Colin turned to me.

"Scouse you've got a susat on your rifle, have a look and if you see the bastards, let them have it." I scanned the horizon of the hill through my scope and very briefly caught sight of them as they bobbed down into cover again.

I turned to Colin.

"Look, there's no fucking way we will catch them by moving over the ground towards them, because there are so many fences and ditches full of water, but there is only one road out of here. Lets move up to the road and cut the bastards off."

"Okay Scouse," he agreed. So we moved off fast, Colin, Skid and me, still trying to stay in cover where possible. Boots and his team stayed put to cover us. We covered the quarter of a mile distance to the road at breakneck speed, my lungs were ready to burst. We stopped the traffic and began a search of all the vehicles. To my bewilderment there was still nothing coming over the radio. By now the Ops room should have sent every man and his dog to assist us, but we had heard nothing.

Searching the line of traffic I got to the fourth vehicle and sat in it were two very worried looking men. I could see that they had been very active within the last few minutes because like us they were still fighting for breath and sweating.

"Out of the car!" I ordered them. They got out of the car and I could see that they were agitated. Skid and Col covered me while I spoke to them. "Where have you just come from?" I asked the driver.

"Just over there," he said pointing in the direction of where we had seen the men on the hill.

"Open the boot," I ordered the driver. He lifted the boot up and inside were two combat rifles and two shotguns and a couple of black woollen hats. I slammed the boot shut and we moved them to the side of the car and Colin summoned the RUC and Boots to our location. Boots arrived first and shortly afterwards the RUC arrived. After the RUC had questioned the men, it was confirmed that their guns were held legally and that they had all the correct paper work. I was disappointed that we hadn't caught two terrorists but the men admitted that they had been shooting on the hill and when they had saw us running they had been frightened. I did not believe a word of their excuse for running away.

This episode left me concerned for two reasons. The first being that the Ops room had missed our contact report (I never found out why), and secondly what would have happened to me if I had opened fire on the two men because irrespective of what Colin or Boots had ordered, it was my finger on the trigger and my arse on the line.

Every day we would patrol for mile after mile in the cold foul weather that seems to be a part of Northern Ireland. We slogged on over fences, through water-filled ditches across rivers where there was no bridge available. We would trample through the fields of cowdung. I lost count of the number of times I felt the belt of an electric current run through me where I had touched an electric fence. During the dark hours it was even worse and we would make painfully slow progress. We would try and suppress a laugh as someone screamed in the pitch black after slipping on a fence and getting the full force between their legs. The one time we did not laugh is when poor Skid slipped from a barbed wire fence cutting his left testicle. Colin radioed the Ops room who didn't try and hide their giggles. Luckily Skid had not done any serious damage.

I suspected there was some favouritism when the patrol rosters were being drawn up because our multiple always seemed to get the midnight shift. On one such patrol we had been dropped by helicopter near the Sperrin Mountains just after midnight. The patrol route was just over seven miles with the normal searches and checks en route. We disembarked from the helicopter to be met by perpetual rain lashing our faces. After an hour or so the rain and wind had increased so much that it was virtually impossible to carry on, we were making no ground at all. We sought refuge in the first barn we came to. It was a unanimous decision to stay put, the helicopter was scheduled to pick us up at seven that morning.

"Right we can stay here till five and then we can move fast to the helicopter pickup," Boots said. Then he added, "fuck it make that four just in case." A stag list was quickly drawn up, one person would stay awake while the rest of us slept. I drew the second watch, which I completed, woke the next guy and then crashed out again.

The next thing I was aware of was an uproar and Boots shouting

"Get up fast. Oh fuck," he was shouting, "we are in the shit!" I checked my watch it was five minutes to seven and five minutes to our helicopter pickup which was over four miles away. Someone had fallen asleep on their stag (we later discovered that the culprit was Milo). Boots had blown a fuse. In the end Colin jumped up and told him to calm down or he would drop him. Then the ingenious plot was hatched. Boots radioed the OP's room and requested that our helicopter pickup be delayed. "Why?" they came back within an instant. Looking a little pale because he was telling a porky, Boots went on to explain that we had spotted a vehicle that was acting suspiciously. Boots gave them a registration number from a vehicle that I had spotted weeks before and a grid reference close to where our pickup would be. They swallowed our story and told us to radio through when we were ready so we set off at breakneck speed towards our destination. It was a nightmare as it was still dark and my knee was more painful than ever. Once we had reached our position Boots, who by now was becoming an accomplished liar, radioed through to the OP's room and said that the vehicle was okay and that it was a false alarm. We were picked up and no one was the wiser. There was a flaw in our plan. If the OP's room had told us to hold the vehicle we would have been in the shit even worse. We had had our last night's sleep in a barn.

The little sleep we were able to get was precious because we were always being woken for some reason, more often than not it was some visiting dignitary from Wales, wanting to get their photographs in the local paper to show how caring they were visiting the poor troops in Northern Ireland. What the pictures didn't say was that we had been dragged from our beds to stand next to these jumped up egocentric prats, so when Mick Parsons shook me awake I thought it was for the usual photo call.

"Scouse," he said, "you're not on patrol tonight so stay in bed."

"Why?" I asked fearing that it must be bad if I was not on patrol.

"I can't say too much, but you're going on a special OP."

"Who with, when and how?" I asked.

"Look, I will brief you properly later," he said, "but it will just be a few of us from our troop and Bags is going too." As soon as Mick left John shouted over from his bed.

"What the fuck's going on, Scouse? How come he said you're not on patrol?"

"I don't know John," I answered, it's some sort of OP, but I don't know myself yet."

All the soldiers chosen for the OP gathered in a small room. Already the smokers had lit their dreaded weed and the smoke drifted in clouds. This really pissed me off because they gave no consideration to us non-smokers. Mick Parsons made his way to the front and stood in front of a hastily arranged blackboard. He called the assembled soldiers to silence.

"I won't drag this out," he said, "I will tell you everything I know and then we shall get on with the job. Here goes," Mick cleared his throat. "We will be part of an operation to mount an OP on the border. Troops from all over Northern Ireland will be taking part so the whole of the border will be monitored. It starts at 23.00 hrs tonight. We will be taken part of the way by helicopter and then we shall have to TAB the remainder. It will last for five days, but here is the good news, we will be getting relieved by a company of the Ulster Defence Regiment on the third night. I warn you now," Mick said. "I want no fuck ups on this, there will be an SAS presence, so stay switched on."

"How far is the TAB from the helicopter?" someone enquired.

"At least five miles," Mick answered, "and it will be over rough terrain and it will be through some densely wooded fire breaks," he added.

There were eight of us who had been picked to go on the OP. Mick Parsons sidled up to me when the others had left the room.

"Look, Scouse, I hope you don't mind but I wanted you on this. Is that okay?" he asked.

"Fine by me Mick," I replied, "in fact I am rather flattered that you trust me. But why Bags?"

Mick hunched his shoulders. "Not my choice."

Each one of us were allocated various amounts of kit to pack in our Bergen's, except, that is Bags. He stood over me smirking as I stowed the radio batteries, food, ammunition and all the other bits and pieces required for an OP.

"Haven't you got anything to carry?" I asked.

"No," he replied.

"In that case why don't you help me then, Bags?" I said.

"Fuck off," he said, "do I look soft?"

Mick Parsons walked over. "Bags," he said, "the only reason I haven't given you anything is because I want you to carry the binoculars and they have very delicate lenses, so come with me and we will go and get them."

"Bags gets the easy job again." I thought. But I was wrong. Mick came back through the door with a huge pair of binoculars. They were at least three feet long and next to the diminutive Bags it looked so funny. Everyone, much to Bags annoyance burst out laughing. The binoculars were so large that they would not fit in a Bergen properly. The last hour we had spare was spent getting as much scoff down us as possible. We covered our faces in camouflage paint and donned our black woollen hats which we would wear for this OP. Contrary to popular belief soldiers in Ulster must adhere to a strict dress code, they are not permitted to wear privately purchased military clothing or carry pathetic Rambo knives with ridiculous compasses on the handle. All that type of rubbish is fine in films or to satisfy the weirdoes who play at soldiers but it's got no part in real soldiering.

Under the cover of darkness we ran from the base and boarded the Puma helicopter which had settled on the grass. It's rotors were still spinning and the reek of aviation fuel saturated the air. We had one final check to make sure all our Bergens were on board and then Mick Parsons gave the loadmaster a thumbs up. Though we were only minutes away from the border our OP position was further along so we would travel parallel with it and then be dropped about five miles short, from where we would TAB the remainder and with luck get in position before the first light and unseen. Every man on board knew that this was going to be a gruelling time. Spending any time in an OP is boring and very uncomfortable and it takes discipline to stay alert. The mind wanders with boredom and before you know it you have nodded off to sleep.

The loadmaster held one finger up indicating we had a minute to landing, I ran my fingers over my rifle to check my magazine was in place. The helicopter landed with a thud, we disembarked and went into routine all round defence of the machine. They are very powerful helicopters Pumas, even so I was surprised to watch it lift off point its nose in the air and start a vertical climb up into the sky. We could neither see or hear it after a minute. We formed up into a staggered line and moved off. Mick Parsons as the boss led the way, once again he had volunteered to come out. The going was fairly easy to begin with and thankfully the rain had held off. Every so often Mick would call a halt while he checked the map. When he did so we would ditch our Bergens and lie our weapons across them just in case we did bump into some active service unit. I could see Bags was struggling with the binoculars but my own Bergen prevented me from helping him. Despite the lack of rain it was a very cold night and when we stopped for any length of time our sweat from humping the heavy Bergens would freeze on our necks and backs. I hated this and so I would curse Mick under my breath when we stopped.

After one such stop we began to move off when my left leg plunged into a slimy water filled hole. I couldn't free myself, the suction of the slime kept hold of my leg. A couple of the guys turned back, freed my Bergen and pulled me out. A few moments later, Bags plunged in up to his waist, then it was Mick's turn. No one escaped a dip into the slime. I was relieved when we eventually turned up a gradient which led us through a fire break in a small wood, but even this was fraught with danger in the form of branches and twigs which littered the ground. A muffled curse would be heard as someone caught their shin on a branch or the clatter as they tripped over and hit the ground. The TAB seemed to go on forever and I was beginning to lose faith in Mick's map reading skills, when he called a halt to tell us we were nearly there.

"How far's nearly Mick?" I asked.

"Just past this wood," he said, and it was just as well

because we still had to set the OP up and get everyone into position before light. True to his word Mick led us in to a small clearing on the edge of the wood. It provided excellent cover. Of the eight man OP six would stay back here to cook and sleep while two men would stay forward and man the actual OP. We would operate a shift system, so many hours on stag and then back to the rear for scoff and sleep. I went forward with Mick and we set about preparing the OP using a ground sheet, a camouflage net and the available vegetation. Blending the oversized binoculars which were coloured white proved to be harder but we managed. Though our purpose was to observe anything suspect in the area our OP did overlook a supposedly obsolete road that ran from the Republic of Ireland to the North. Part of the road we had been told was under water after the Army had bombed it to prevent its use. The OP finished, I rigged a handset up and trailed a communications line, concealing it as I did so, back to the rear admin area. Mick drew the stag list up and those who were able to got some sleep in the rear admin area.

Four men would sleep while two manned the radios from base and the line from the OP up front. I woke up to Bags telling me that he and I were up front next. We got some scoff and moved up to relieve the two lads on stag. As always on OP's if possible there should be no movement, but if there is it should be kept to a minimum and be done quietly. Things look very different in the light of day and the OP wasn't in the perfect cover I had thought it was. I had my first glance through the binoculars at the old road. Far from being unused, cars were crossing it at a few an hour, only slowing their vehicles to ford the water. We logged every registration and that was it. We lay there freezing our nuts off. I didn't expect to see masses of IRA walking over the border, but there wasn't a flicker of anything even remotely interesting.

On the third night Mick Parsons summoned me to go with him to rendezvous with the UDR soldiers who would be taking over from us. This time we had no Bergens to carry so it would be easier. I took a couple of spare magazines just in case. The RV was just short of where we had originally been dropped by the helicopter. Even without our Bergens it was still a pain in the arse stepping into the bogs and tripping over fallen trees. We arrived at the RV with time to spare and Mick radioed our position to base, so we sat there and waited and waited. I was getting cold and rather pissed off.

"Those bastards have got lost," I said to Mick.

"No," he replied, "they are just slow." We had been issued chemical heat pads for the OP. They are an excellent piece of kit that resemble the small bean bags used by infant school children in the gym. To activate the pads, a drop of water is poured through a small hole in the neck and then shaken mixing the chemicals and the water and this produces heat for hours at a time. As we sat there in the darkness freezing I regretted not bringing one with me.

"Mick we should have made the RV with them by now," I said.

"What do you suggest I do Scouse?" Mick asked.

"Get on the radio and confirm our position and get them to confirm theirs," I said.

Rather reluctantly Mick reeled off our position on the radio and he was told to wait. Moments later we were informed that the UDR soldiers were waiting for us and they were in the wrong position a mile and a half away.

"Stay at your position," we were ordered "and we will send them to you."

"I fucking knew it Mick," I gloated, "the tossers got lost."

We sat there for a further half hour, then I heard talking and metal clacking against metal. I began to feel uneasy.

"That can't be them, Mick," I whispered, "surely they would not be so stupid to make such a racket."

"I don't know," he replied, "go forward and challenge them."

"Me!" I protested.

"Yes, you, Scouse, I am the staff sergeant." I kept low and moved along the track towards the direction of the noise, Mick promised to provide cover and I trusted him. In the darkness I could make out two figures both of them smoking, each time they took a drag on their cigarettes their faces glowed. They were chatting like buddies who had met in a bar laughing and joking. My fear now was not that they were IRA because no terrorist would betray his presence like these two characters, but they might think I was. I decided to get it over with.

"Army," I shouted.

"Hello, there," came the cheerful reply "we're UDR." They walked over and shook me by the hand. It was pointless me trying to explain the need for stealth and a few other points in the art of soldiering, for one thing I was out-ranked and also these soldiers lived here.

"Where's the rest of your men?" I asked one of the UDR soldiers he gave a short whistle and another six UDR soldiers came out of the darkness as did Mick behind me. Mick and I stood open-mouthed when we saw that they were carrying calor gas bottles and folding beds, it looked more like they were heading for a trip to the beach.

"Are you taking the piss fellas?" Mick asked them.

"No," one of them replied, "we just like our comforts."

"But its a fucking OP you're doing."

"So what?" was the reply. They humped and bumped all their rubbish over the five miles to the OP. We passed over command and fucked off fast to our helicopter pick up. I was fit to drop when we returned to base.

I was in quite a bit of pain with my knee after the OP so I asked to see a doctor. The result was I was given the once over by a field medic, given some pain killers and laughing at his own joke the medic said "rest it".

Our nocturnal wanderings around the border continued, we were always paired up with Boots' team and I had grown to trust them all, but a few weeks after the OP we had cause to pass through Strabane on foot patrol. It was not really our task to stop any of the locals because we were now working out of Castlederg. None of us, though, could resist the temptation of stopping the local low-life just to give them some hassle. Miles had stopped a lad and we never took too much notice until Milo blew his stack. He began to scream and shout at the lad and I thought for a moment Milo was going to stick one on him. He was bawling so loudly that a crowd began to gather around. Boots and Duncan wisely intervened and told the lad to move on. Milo acted as though nothing had happened and I looked on bewildered by his sudden change of personality. This little incident left me worried because I had thought Milo was quite an unassuming lad.

On one particularly dull and boring 24 hour patrol after being turned away by Mrs O we decided to give her daughter Tracy a visit. This was a one-off because of the distance between their homes, but we thought it would be worth the hike. Tracy was just as obliging as her mother in the tea and cakes department. Anything else on offer was being taken care of by a soldier from another patrol and the same applied to her friend who was there on this visit. Tracy gave us a much longer lead than her mother and soldiers being soldiers we took full advantage of it. We would request videos and she would go and hire them for us and bring back cakes and goodies for us to eat. These girls had a captive audience in us and they loved it. I loved just being in a normal home away from the barracks. Tracy would let me use her toilet where I could crap in peace without the grunts of a soldier in the next cubical trying to conjure images of women from the sticky porn magazines that had been left in the toilets by the previous regiment. If we called during the dark hours and Tracy wasn't home we would hang around in her shed waiting for her to return. This was a far cry from the caution we took when we first arrived and this skiving wasn't unique to just our teams, all the soldiers were at it. We knew it was wrong and very dangerous, even to the people we visited, but the Army had to take some of the blame because of the conditions they imposed on us. They were fully aware that this type of skiving went on, but they had no idea to what extent.

One cold dark night we were patrolling down an isolated country lane when we came across a small house and Colin told us that it was the home of a player. All terrorists in Northern Ireland were referred to as players, why I don't know, because it certainly wasn't a game we were playing. Colin told John, who was carrying a very powerful torch to shine it in to the bedroom window of the terrorists house to try and wake him up. I was all for giving these scum a hard time, but judging by the thick blackout curtains hanging from the windows this was nothing new to the player who lived there. After some fifteen minutes of this game I was starting to get bored and cold and I said to John, "This is a fucking waste of time."

Colin came running over to me. "I am the brick commander here not you," he said.

"I know you're the fucking brick commander," I replied, "but this is a fucking waste of time, we could be getting on with some real patrolling. Can't you see we are all freezing our fucking balls off standing around here and for all you know the bastard might not even be at home."

"I don't give a shit." Colin said and to prove a point we stayed there a while longer.

A bit later on into the patrol we stopped at a barn to make a brew and Colin came over to me.

"Scouse, I am the commander of this team and if I want to hassle the players I will," he reiterated.

"I know you're the commander of our team," I repeated, "but as we are a team, I thought that meant we were supposed to work together and if we weren't happy with something we could say."

"Yes you can," he said, "but you were trying to criticise my order."

"I wasn't," I answered, "I just thought it was a fucking waste of time so I said so. Look, if you are not happy with the way I work then if you want I will ask if I can be moved to another team when we get back." This was a bluff I didn't want to move to another team away from John and Skid. Colin, realising that he would be out of favour with John and Skid, said "No, Scouse I want you in our team, you know your job, its just that I wasn't happy with the way you moaned over shining the light through the bedroom window." I felt guilty now because I had called his bluff and it had worked.

"I'm sorry," I said, "next time I will keep my mouth shut." Colin tapped me on the back. "No hard feelings," he said.

"No," I replied. Arguments seemed to break out over the most ridiculous things. I saw two of the lads nearly come to blows one night as to how one of the whores back in Germany pronounced Milan.

"She says Milano", one of them was shouting.

"She says fucking Milan," the other screamed, "and I should know because I have fucked her more than you."

During one patrol we were all pissed off because an officer had decided to accompany us. Why this captain had chosen to leave the cosy confines of the barracks and rough it with us low-life soon became apparent, when halfway through the patrol he produced his camera and asked us to take some happy snaps of him.

"Where do we sneak off for a brew?" he asked thinking we had accepted him as one of the boys because he had joined us for a patrol. No one answered him so we just carried on patrolling at a blistering rate to show him how hard it was. We waded through the rivers in the regulation manner climbed the fences and generally made the patrol as hard as possible. Our plan worked and by the time we returned to the base the captain was ready to drop and he never came out with us again.

There is a garage near Castlederg and as we patrolled past it in the dead of night, John and I noticed that the door leading to the showroom was slightly ajar. We silently alerted the rest of the patrol and quick as a flash they moved in to position to give us covering fire. To the outsider this course of action may have seemed rather dramatic but the reality is that we may have stumbled on an IRA active service unit in the process of planting an explosive device and caution was paramount. It may have been that the owner had simply forgotten to lock up properly but we could not take any risks. John and I crept closer making no sound. John stood on one side of the plate glass window and I stood the other side both of us out of sight. John had a nightvision sight attached to his rifle. This brilliant piece of equipment allowed us to view in the dark. The only drawback with it was the whistling sound it made when it was switched on. It wasn't very loud but in the dead of night it was exaggerated. I signalled to John to take a peek through the sight. He switched it on bobbed his head round had a scan and then moved back in to cover. He raised two fingers indicating that there were two people inside. John beckoned me over so I stooped down out of sight and moved over to him. He put his mouth close to my ear and whispered.

"There are two of them inside," he said "and they are just pilfering stuff from the office."

"Okay John," I whispered, "you cover them with the sight and I will shout to them that we have seen them and there is no escape." I moved over and told Boots what was happening as he was the senior commander on the ground with us and then I moved back over to John. We had only seen two men, but we had to assume that there could be more on the premises.

"Okay, are you ready, John?" I whispered.

"Okay," he replied.

"This is the army come out!" I shouted.

"They're hiding in the corner," John said, "they don't realise we can see them."

"Come out now or we will come in!" I shouted.

"We're scared," came the reply.

"I don t give a fuck," I answered. "Come out now or we're coming in to get you and you will be sorry."

"Okay, we are coming out," came the reply. The two men walked out of the door with a resigned look on their faces. John grabbed hold of one of the men and I got hold of his accomplice.

"Raise your arms while I search you," I ordered my prisoner. He offered no resistance, but I was quite sure if this had been in the middle of the day they would have played to the crowd. I found a number of cassettes and small change and some spark plugs on the lad I was holding. John's prisoner had so much loose change on him I was surprised he could walk with the weight of it all.

"Where did all this money come from, the charity boxes?" I enquired.

"No you have got it all wrong, its me uncle's garage and we were just cleaning it out," said the lad I was holding.

"Cleaning it out is about right," I said, "but I don't for one second believe it's your uncle's."

An unmarked police car arrived and I assumed that either Boots or Colin had radioed for it but in fact it had just been passing and one of our lads had waved it down. The three policemen who got out of the car recognised the two prisoners straight away. They put the two lads into the police car and we walked the short distance to the police station to give our statements. The rest of the patrol were chuffed as this meant we would spend the rest of the night at the station giving statements while they slept. We soon learned that the lads were brothers and by the morning they had been charged with nine burglaries including four they had committed that night. The police were elated that we had caught them at it, but it really was just good luck. Ironically, our efforts this night would mean John and I returning to Northern Ireland some time later.

14

The NITAT team had prepared us well for Northern Ireland. The training they had given us was very realistic, if not a little over-exaggerated, but as the floods in Strabane had proven there are some events that can happen that are not written on the pages of any Army training manual and the events of this day were certainly never covered in our training.

Colin Roberts was away on four days R and R, so John King although only a gunner, had been given command of the brick. John had discussed this with me and Skid asking if we minded. We were both happy for him to do it. A soldier called Karl Jones had moved in to our team to make the numbers up while Colin was away. Karl was an easy going lad and he made a joke about everything, he always had a smile on his face, and I was happy to have him in our team. We had been tasked to patrol up to the border, checking roads on the way for any signs of IRA booby traps in the form of wires leading to any points where explosives could be planted, to attack a police or Army patrol. It was a thankless task because it meant that we would have to trudge through the fields that ran parallel with the roads, looking for anything concealed beneath the mud and cow shit. Boots, who still had overall command of our multiple patrol, came into the Portacabin still looking half asleep.

"Okay," he shouted trying to sound authoritative, "we will

be going out by helicopter at six am so be ready." Sometimes we would leave the base by helicopter even if it meant we were only going a short distance. This was so that we never built up any pattern of leaving the base at any particular time or by any particular method. It was all intended to fool the IRA, but I wasn't convinced we were fooling them.

I checked my watch. It was just after five so we had plenty of time.

"What time are we back in, Boots?" I asked him.

"Just after dinner time Scouse," he replied, "so its only a short patrol, thank fuck."

I stowed all the gear and equipment I would need for the patrol into my Bergen. I then checked my weapon over to make sure it was spotlessly clean and I gave my scope a polish. I lay back on my bed and watched all the other lads going about their business. They knew if they needed help they only had to say. It was the same for us all. It was a well practiced routine now we each knew what had to be done before and after each patrol. Weapons had to be cleaned and checked, combats washed and dried, boots dried and polished. Reports had to be written out and given to the collator. Radio batteries had to be changed. There would be no sleep or food after a patrol until all these things had been done and no one slacked until they had.

Duncan, who could sleep on a washing line, was dossing on his bed. John was getting some last minute advice off Boots about being a team commander. I looked over to Milo who was sitting on his bed with headphones on listening to music on his personal stereo. I was concerned about Milo and I had even spoken to Trev Lovejoy about his behaviour. Milo had taken to cleaning the toilets after each patrol. He hadn't been ordered to do this and that's what worried me. Trev Lovejoy had brushed my concerns aside.

"He is just a bit stressed out that's all," he said.

Looking over at Milo I felt it was more than stress. We

were all under stress but none of us had the desire to go and clean the toilets after each patrol. I put my fears to the back of my mind and closed my eyes.

"Scouse come on move." It was John waking me up. "We have got ten minutes till the helicopter," he said. I got off my bed and woke Skid who was also asleep. We moved out to the perimeter fence and sat and waited for the helicopter. The sky was dark with a threat of rain, but for the moment it was dry. John was flapping like a mother hen asking us if we were okay. I resisted the temptation to tell him that the tour was almost over and at this stage of the game we all knew what we had to do and what kit we needed to patrol. It was rather pointless John trying to impress the bosses anyway because he would be leaving the Army on our return to Germany which was only a matter of weeks away. John, like many soldiers, had become very disillusioned with the Army. It was a shame because he was a fine soldier.

As usual the helicopter was late and so to kill the boredom we started telling jokes and taking the piss out of each other. Everyone was laughing, everyone that is except Milo, who had a very strange expression on his face, one of anger and fear. He caught my eye as I looked at him and it sent a shiver up my spine. In that moment I knew that there was something very wrong with Milo and for the first time I felt fearful of him. While the others laughed and joked my thoughts turned to the realisation that Milo had a weapon fully loaded with twenty high velocity rounds and another spare magazine of twenty rounds just for good measure.

Boots cracked a joke and Milo's face broke into a huge grin.

Maybe it's me that's under stress, I thought, I am reading in to this things that are not there. Milo is probably just tired like the rest of us. The helicopter bumped down on to the grass and we ran and boarded in a well-rehearsed fashion. Boots passed on the grid reference to the pilot and he banked the aircraft towards our destination. I always enjoyed the helicopter rides, I would look out of the window as the fields and rivers below slipped by with ease. Fields and rivers that took us so many hours of hard work to cover by foot. I would gaze at the pilot with envy wishing that I had got myself an education and been able to fly these machines, but as always my dreams would end as we leaped out of the door in some barren field that was Northern Ireland. The helicopter flew away and we stood in silence checking our equipment.

"Okay," Boots said pointing to a long road in the distance, "that is the road we will be doing the route check on, basically looking for wires either side of it."

After trudging to the road John asked Boots which side he wanted our team to check.

"Take your pick," Boots said with a smile because one side of the road was very muddy and boggy.

"Fuck it," John said laughing, "we are hard as fuck, we will do the muddy side."

Milo interrupted "No, you're not. We're doing the muddy side aren't we?" he said fixing Boots with an icy stare.

"What are you trying to be, a martyr?" I said to Milo instantly regretting my words.

"We are doing it," he said a little louder. As he climbed over the fence we stared at each other in amazement, if not with a little embarrassment. Boots shrugged his shoulders. "If that's what he wants," he said and followed him.

John and I, and the remainder of our team began our check on the opposite side of the road. We walked parallel with Boots and his team and kept watching Milo with more than a little interest. Knowing he was out of ear shot John moved close to me "What do you reckon, Scouse?" he said.

"Well," I replied, "he is losing it and we have two choices we fuck off back in now and report him or we just carry on and watch him."

"We'll watch him," John said.

We completed the route check and took cover at the side of the road.

"Okay let's get some scoff!" Boots shouted to everyone. We had been given a cold lunch of sandwiches and sausage rolls because it was a fairly short patrol. Pouring myself some coffee from my flask, I glanced over to see Boots and John had crawled up a nearby bank and were watching something in a field. Curiosity got the better of me, so I moved over to get a look myself.

"What's up John?" I said sliding down next to him.

"Oh its these two." he replied in a hushed tone pointing towards two men in the middle of the field. The two men John had pointed to were stood in the middle of the recently ploughed field, each of them had a spade, but neither of them wore wellington boots or indeed dress as the farmers did or at least the ones we had come to know during our time in Northern Ireland.

"Would they be so obvious?" I whispered to John.

"Or so cheeky?" he replied.

"Point taken." I moved back over to finish my feast but as I did so it began to rain. I dug in to my backpack and pulled out my waterproof jacket. John and Boots did not move they were very interested in the two men in the field. I looked over at Milo, he was rummaging into his pocket for something. I returned to my food. A few moments later the sound of pop music filled the air we all jumped to our feet in surprise.

"What the fuck!?" Boots shouted out. I looked over to see Milo with his Dictaphone which we used to record vehicle registration numbers held to his ear dancing round. He had obviously recorded some music on to it.

"Fucking turn the thing off" Boots shouted. Milo spun round facing Boots. When I saw Milo's face, the hairs on the back of my neck stood up and I pulled my rifle towards me.

His eyes were wide and staring and his jaw was jutted out. He looked not only aggressive but very frightening.

"No I won't!" he shouted at Boots. Boots quite rightly realised that something had snapped in Milo. We all did, except Duncan, who was at the far end of the bank still eating his scoff.

"Okay," Boots said in a calm voice trying to pacify Milo.

"No I fucking won't!" Milo screamed. This was now starting to look dangerous. My heart was pounding.

"It's okay Milo, mate," I said, "Boots wasn't having a go at you was you, Boots?"

"Nnno," Boots stammered. Mistake. Milo spun round fixing me with his bulging eyes.

"You've made it rain haven't you" he said. Now he had his rifle pointing at me. For one mad second I considered jumping him.

"Scouse, didn't make it rain," Karl said trying to pacify Milo and in doing so he put himself in danger. The most important and worrying thought was whether Milo had cocked his weapon. If he had this would mean he would only have to release his safety catch and he could start firing and without a doubt he would kill at least some of us and to make matters worse none of us were wearing body armour because it was impossible to wear on rural patrolling.

Milo turned his attentions back to Boots.

"Lets go in to Southern Ireland," he said rather matter of factly.

"Okay," Boots replied and stood up. Milo moved closer to him with his rifle pointing rather dangerously at his head. Boots was obviously playing it cool. Karl, Skid, John and me fell in behind them staying at a safe distance.

"What the fuck are we going to do now?" John said in a state of panic. There was no way we could let Milo forcibly take Boots and his team over the Irish border which was only a mile or so away. There are numerous political problems when soldiers cross the border into the Republic of Ireland, even if by accident through a map reading error! If asked British soldiers must surrender their weapons under protest to the Garda or Irish Army. What if Milo was challenged. Would he fire on them? If so it would be a bloodbath. I cocked my weapon out of earshot of Milo.

"What about the radio?" John asked.

"Lets inform the Ops room now and see what they think we should do." But we realised if we did then Milo would hear on Boots' radio. We then decided to try one of our alternative frequencies and it worked. John informed the Ops room of our desperate situation they replied immediately 'WAIT OUT.'

I knew now that they would be running around like headless chickens wondering what to do. I felt angry because Milo's odd behaviour had been brought to their attention and they had dismissed it as nothing to worry about. All the time we were moving closer to the border as we waited for them to come back with a decision.

I asked John who, technically speaking, was my commander. "What shall we do if Milo begins firing or even worse suddenly slots Boots?"

John looked at me with an expression of sheer fear on his face. "Well, Scouse, you're the only one who has a sussat scope on your rifle."

"What are you saying John, that you want me to shoot him if he opens fire?"

John nodded. "What the fuck else can we do Scouse? He has flipped his lid."

"Okay John," I said trying to sound positive "I just wanted to hear it from you."

"I will take the blame if you want, Scouse, just take him out if he harms anybody," John said with more determination in his voice.

"John, I don't want you to take any blame as long as you're behind me if I have to," I said.

"Of course I fucking am," John replied.

I was scared. We were all scared because we were contemplating the shooting of a fellow British soldier, one of our own. I knew if I had to shoot Milo he would surely die. Shooting to wound is fiction, you aim at the centre of the body and, given the awesome firepower of the SLR, I was carrying it would be like hitting a water melon with a sledge hammer. I also had to consider the other members of Boots team. If Milo did start shooting, what would they do? I could not risk killing one of them.

To the casual observer our multiple patrol looked like any other. No-one could possibly guess the situation we were in. I swept the surrounding countryside with the sussat on my rifle as I did on all patrols but this time my real intention was to keep a check on Milo. The activities of the two men who had been acting suspiciously in the field was no longer important although we did have a grid reference of where they had been.

Finally the Ops room came back on the radio to us. It was quite rightly decided that it would be far too risky to send out a helicopter or any police as they may well have been enough to make Milo start firing. What they were going to do was send out a bogus message on the radio to Boots saying that we all had to return back to base on the pretence of changing radio batteries. It was a weak plan but what else could we do? They also said that our route back to the base would be kept clear. We switched back to Boots' channel and the message came through. I watched through my sussat as Milo and Boots stopped and started talking, then they began to double back.

"I think its worked John." I said. But John didn't seem convinced. As Boots came within ear shot, he shouted to John that we had to return to base to change our radio batteries.

"Oh for fucks sake!" John replied pretending to sound pissed off. As Boots passed he gave us a knowing look and once again we fell in behind them while keeping our distance.

As we began the intense walk back to base John shouted over to me.

"What the fuck's up with him, Scouse?"

"I don't know John." I replied, "but he's finished here, they won't let him out on the streets again." I kept a close watch on Milo for any signs that he was about to kick off. The worst moments began when we had the base in sight, but Milo did nothing and we patrolled in as normal. However I did notice the normally busy unloading bay was deserted. We all unloaded our weapons making sure that Milo had unloaded first. Mick Parsons and a senior officer appeared and Milo was led away. We never saw him again. We were later informed that Milo was suffering from some form of mental illness and we were also praised at our handling of a very dangerous situation. It was sad because we had lost Milo, but at least we had been spared the agony of shooting a fellow soldier.

Milo's possessions were quickly packed and taken away and we continued to patrol, but the whole incident had left us shocked. John King had turned out to be a very good commander and he gained my respect. He had been under enormous pressure that day, but he had made a decision and in doing so had put his own neck on the line. I have seen far more experienced men buckle under less demanding circumstances.

As our Northern Ireland tour was drawing to an end the advanced party from 19 Field Regiment Royal Artillery began to arrive. Their soldiers would then join ours on patrol so they could get to know the ground before the main body of the regiment arrived. It was a very vulnerable time for all concerned because the IRA was fully aware that there was a change over in progress despite our attempts to conceal it.

Sadly 19 Field Regiment were to suffer a loss of one soldier and injuries to other soldiers on their tour.

On our very last patrol we were dropped by helicopter near the border in the late afternoon with a scheduled helicopter pick-up at midnight. Colin Roberts was now back in charge of our team, but once again we were with Boots and his team only this time Milo had been replaced with Karl Jones.

"Right hands up those in favour of doing fuck all and skiving." Boots said with a smile. Seven hands shot up. "Okay," Boots said, "unfortunately we are too far away to give Mrs O a final visit, so we will have to make do with her lovely daughter Tracy."

We arrived at Tracy's to find her mate Ann's car in the drive.

"Good she is in then." Boots said.

We used the same routine as at Mrs O's. Boots knocked on the door asking if he could search the garden. Tracy gave him the nod and we all slipped in through the back door. Ann was still sitting there in her dressing gown looking rather dejected.

"What's up with you?" I asked her.

"The love of my life is leaving," she said referring to a soldier from our troop.

"She is like this every time the regiments change over," Tracy said laughing. I wondered if she realised that the soldiers were just using her and once the tour was over so was she, but on the other hand she had a captive audience, she could pick and choose which must have been a real morale booster because she was no oil painting.

We sat there all evening eating cakes and drinking tea, until at 10.30 pm Boots told us to start getting our kit together as we had a three mile walk to the helicopter pick up. None of us felt guilty about staying there all evening, it was the last patrol and we were even more fearful of getting hit than usual. We put our backpacks on and picked our weapons up and

NOT FOR QUEEN AND COUNTRY

started to say our goodbyes to Tracy and Ann. Boots pulled the curtain back to have a quick look outside the front of the house.

"Oh fuck," he said stepping back "Oh fuck," he repeated. "What's up Boots?" we all began to ask panicking.

"The fucking police are outside the house doing vehicle checks. We're in the shit." Boots said, "Or rather," correcting himself, "I am in the shit." John began to laugh more because of the absurdity of the situation we were in. Boots turned on him "Its not fucking funny!"

"I know, Boots," John said, "but I can't help it."

"Instead of laughing try and think of what we are going to do," Boots said. '

'How about if we just walk out the door and if they ask say we were just searching the house," someone piped in.

"No, it will never work," Boots said.

"Well, we are stuck here till they go," I said, "we will just have to wait."

There was no chance of slipping out the back door because they most certainly had an officer at the side of the house. Watching over the guy stopping the cars as the minutes slipped by we were becoming more agitated. Then the arguing started.

"Whose fucking idea was it to come here anyway?" Boots said.

"It was your idea." Colin shouted back.

"All right, all right!" John shouted, "shut the fuck up or they will hear us arguing and that won't solve anything."

We even considered using the old trick of saying we had seen something to delay the helicopter, but then what if they decided to send in the policemen who were outside the house?

Finally at 11.20 pm the policemen moved off.

"We will never make it across all those fields," Boots said in a voice that suggested that he was resigned to his fate.

"What if I take you in my car?" Ann said. Boots dropped his jaw and then looked to us for a reaction.

"Fuck it," we all agreed, "it's our only chance."

"You will never fit us all in" Boots said now in total despair.

"I know that you soft bastard," Ann replied, "I can take four of you then come back for the others, but we will have to go now."

Boots made his mind up in a second he knew that it was our only hope.

They all squeezed in to Ann's clapped out car, but to us at this moment it was a golden chariot. The car spluttered out of the driveway and we began the tense wait.

"What if they get stopped?" said Skid.

"Then we are in the shit," Karl replied. After what seemed to be forever Ann's car spluttered up the drive and with a quick goodbye to Tracy we all ran out and piled in to it.

"Did it go all right?" Karl asked Ann.

"It's okay," she said, "stop ya worrying."

"Okay," he said, "lets fucking move, we have only 15 minutes to midnight."

We set off along the dark country roads towards the pickup. As he was the team commander we made Colin sit in the front, while Skid, John and me sat in the back. We had our rifles propped up between our legs and our backpacks on our knees. The stupidity of what we were doing hit me. If we were now stopped by an illegal IRA checkpoint it would be impossible to bring our weapons to bear and also they would certainly kill Ann for her fraternisation.

The heater was on full and I was sweating so much it felt like I had run the three miles.

"Ann, thanks for this," Colin said, "you have saved our bacon we can't tha . . ." he stopped mid sentence. "Oh shit!" I felt a surge of fear run through me even before I had looked up and I felt no better when I did. Ahead of us someone stood in the road circling a red torch. This was a signal used by police and troops to stop vehicles. It has also known to be used by the IRA.

"What should I do?" Ann screamed in panic.

"Keep going very slowly" Colin said.

I tried frantically to pull my weapon free but it was impossible with the limited space. I was also hampered by our backpacks.

"It's the fucking RUC!" Colin shouted.

"Oh fucking shit!" Skid said, "we are truly in the shit now."

"What the fuck are you going to do, Colin?" asked John.

"What the fuck can I do!" he replied. "We are all in deep shit, because they won't miss this opportunity of dropping us in it."

Even before the car had stopped I was contemplating the fine or possible term in a military prison that would surely follow. The car drew to a halt and a policeman made his way cautiously around to the driver's side where Anne had already lowered her window.

"Good evening may I see your driv . . . What the fuck aarr you? Regulars?" he spluttered as his torch beam swept across the four soldiers sitting in the car.

"Yes, we are regulars." Colin answered waiting for the policeman to order us out of the car.

"Oh eerr . . . okay?" the stunned policeman replied "Off you go lads." We sped off in to the darkness.

"I don't fucking believe it," I said. "We have made it."

"He must have thought we were SAS." Skid said. We all burst out laughing with relief at our good luck.

We arrived at the road close to where the helicopter was due to pick us up. Boots and the rest of his team came out of the shadows.

"Where the fuck have you been?" he said, "its gone fucking midnight."

"We got stopped by the RUC." Colin shouted. I could hear Boots give an audible gasp of horror.

"You are fucking joking," he said.

"Honest Boots," Colin said, "the RUC stopped us, but they didn't take our names or details and let us go."

When Boots eventually calmed down we managed to convince him that we had got away with it by the skin of our teeth. We bade our farewells to Anne and she drove off no doubt wondering about her next affair with the new batch of soldiers who would be taking over from us. We moved into the field and a few minutes later the helicopter cluttered down from the dark skies and landed. We ran forward, the sweet smell of the aviation fuel and the warm blast from the engine enveloping us as we slid the door back and climbed in. I loved these moments after a patrol, when we could sit in the back of the helicopter gazing at the glow of the instrument panel while frozen hands and feet thawed out in the warmth. The pilots never even tried to engage us in conversation. For them we were just cargo that they had to move around and to us they were just a form of transport, a glorified taxi.

On a wet and windy Belfast afternoon we all boarded a plane bound for RAF Gutasloh Germany. John sat next to me looking a little pale. He was suffering the effects of a huge hangover having got himself well and truly drunk the previous night. I had come to know John well over the last year and I would sorely miss him as he was due to leave the Army on our return to Germany and it was the Army's loss to be losing such a good soldier. As we sat there waiting for the plane to take off, I thought back to the day we had arrived in Northern Ireland and I shuddered at how naive we had been. We had all been through so much but I was none the wiser as to what solutions there were for peace. The hatred runs too deep in the communities and while the IRA hold the people in fear nothing can really change. I felt, and still do, that the nationalists hatred for the British borders on the insane. They blame the British for all their ills and they always will even if they achieve their goal of getting a united Ireland. Northern Ireland is not a war zone, its much worse than that.

15

After all the formalities and necessary paper work were completed Skid and I reported back to T Battery, 12 Regiment. John had simply handed in his kit and left, he was now a civilian. Skid and I waited outside the BSM's office door, he had told the BSM of 35 Battery that he wanted to see the both of us on our return. I had a fair idea why, because 12 Regiment was about to embark on a tour of Northern Ireland and they were due to start training and I knew the BSM was going to ask me if I wanted to accompany them. I had the right to refuse, because having just returned I was entitled to certain period of time not engaged on active service. I had already made my mind up that I would go back with them, but the problem with my knees was worse than ever and I was now in some considerable pain. Thus, ultimately, the decision would lie with the medical officer as to whether I went back or not. Skid was also due to leave the Army, so it was out of the question that he would go back.

The BSM opened his door and called Skid and I in to his office.

"Right," he said sitting himself down, "I haven't received your reports from 22 Regiment yet, but I have spoken to the BC of 35 Battery and he has told me that all of you were a credit to T Battery, so well done. Now, you are fully aware that we are about to commence training for our own tour of

Northern Ireland?" Skid gave a nervous cough. "Its okay Powell, I realise you are due to leave the Army," the BSM said," but I was wondering; would you like to join us for the tour Denmark?" he added turning to me.

"Yes, sir I would," I replied, "but I have got to see the MO this afternoon because of a knee injury so I would like to see what he says first."

"Okay," the BSM said, "if he passes you fit then I will assume that you are with us."

"Yes sir," I replied. The BSM was a good boss who was always willing to listen when on the right side of him, but if a soldier crossed him it was a different story. I had been marched in to his office once for fighting in the accommodation block while drunk. As I had stood before him with two black eyes and swollen lips trying not to faint because a huge hangover he had screamed at me that it was just as well my eyes were blackened because it had saved him the job of doing it. After such a dressing down with him he would not hold it against you. Once he had given his punishment be it extra guard duties or his favourite gardening detail, which involved digging the same patch of soil over and over, he would not mention it again.

As I made my way over to my room in the accommodation block I met lads from the troop whom I hadn't seen for months. They were all brimming with enthusiasm over the coming tour of Northern Ireland, like I had been when I had started training with 35 Battery, but now I realised that I couldn't feel the same way about this tour. I knew that I would have trouble going along with the exaggerated training which I would be compelled to do all over again despite having just returned. I now half regretted saying yes to the BSM about accompanying T Battery. I hadn't told the BSM, but I had also signed off while in Northern Ireland and if I was honest with myself it was because they had done little or nothing over my knee trouble while there. I caught up with

Mac in the room and by coincidence he had also signed off, meaning we would leave the Army around the same time once more. Mac had also been to Northern Ireland with another regiment, but he had returned before Christmas and so by rights he should have accompanied T Battery but somehow he talked his way out of it. He recounted the moment when he had told the BSM that didn't want to go back. The BSM had started off calmly trying to coax him, but realising his efforts were in vain he then lost his temper and chased Mac around his office threatening to kill him. It ended with the BSM telling Mac he was going and that was that. Mac then played his ace card and went to see the regimental padre to whom he had poured out all his troubles and pretend fears about having to go back to Ireland which wasn't fair because he had not long been back. The padre then went to see the BSM and the end result was Mac was told he didn't have to go. Never underestimate the powers of the regimental padre. Mac wisely stayed out of the BSM's way.

The decision on me going back to Northern Ireland was taken out of my hands that afternoon. The MO, after examining my knees, had said it was out of the question that I return to Ireland and I was told to see an orthopaedic surgeon the following day. The BSM, in contrast to how he had been with Mac, was very sympathetic when I told him the outcome, which meant I didn't have to run around his desk with my sore knees.

The orthopaedic surgeon at Munster military hospital injected steroids in to my knees and told me to go easy and refrain from doing too much, but this advice fell on deaf ears when I returned to the barracks, because Mac informed me that he and I were to help the NITAT team in the Northern Ireland training for the regiment. We were fitted out with uniforms supplied by the RUC, so during the day we would take on the role of policemen and of a night time we would act as terrorists. Somehow in between all this we would have to try and get some sleep. I decided to give my help in the training all the enthusiasm it deserved because it is a serious business, and I also realised that I still had just under a year to go before leaving the Army and once the regiment had left for Ireland and I was left with the rear party the only thing I could look forward to was endless guard duties, interspersed with the boring and tedious servicing and cleaning of vehicles and equipment. The prospects for the coming year looked depressing.

The training began and we gave them the run about without mercy. I knew all the tricks. Part of the barracks had been made to look like a typical Northern Irish housing estate, all designed to get the lads into the right frame of mind. All the training staff operated from the regiment's training wing, which was out of bounds to the troops, so we could plot attacks in peace and after planting our mock explosives or shooting one of the soldiers, we could run back there to safety, if we were not caught. Like all the regiments while in training, they were blind to our little traps at first. They were walking past weapons and command wires that led to simulated explosive devices. Our attacks were so obvious it would have been hard not have seen them coming, but alas, as had happened with us, their brains kicked in to gear and they began to hamper our attacks on them.

During our play acting one incident left me a little concerned. I was playing the role of an awkward thug, the type who are abundant in Northern Ireland. I was stopped by a patrol who I did not know, because like I had done they had come from another regiment and were accompanying 12 Regiment on the tour.

"I am going to search you," the patrol commander said very aggressively. I gave the age old response that I had always received when searching somebody.

"Under what section?" I asked. The patrol commander and his men should have known that it was Section 12 of the

Prevention of Terrorism Act 1978 and that this should always be quoted when about to carry out a search.

"I don't know," he replied.

"Well you ain't searching me until you do fucking know," I said.

"I am going to fucking search you!" he shouted. Already I could see that he was losing his temper and looking flustered. He had left himself wide open, because he had shown a lack of knowledge for his job, but even worse he had lost his cool.

"You are not searching me until I know what section," I spat back.

"I don't fucking know!" he screamed at me. This lad had already fucked up but now he was digging himself even further in to a hole by admitting that he didn't know the regulation by which he was governed. He had not even bothered to ask a member of his patrol who could possibly have told him. If this lad were to act like this in a real situation they would eat him for breakfast.

"Put your fucking arms up you, you bastard!" he screamed and stuttered.

"No!" I shouted back. Without warning he raised his rifle and started screaming.

"Put your arms up or I will smash your fucking head in you bastard."

"No," I repeated, "not until you have told me what section." He was now shaking and his face was glowing red. He lowered his rifle spun around on his heels and walked off calling his team to follow him. They all stood there open-mouthed at his performance. I chased after him and told him that I would be reporting him to the NITAT training team.

"Why?" he asked looking puzzled. "Is it because I didn't know under what section I could search you." I tried to explain to him that it wasn't normal procedure to stand in the street bawling and shouting, and further that raising your rifle was not the thing to do. I did report the soldier, but as far as I know he did go to Northern Ireland.

The training over, 12 Regiment embarked on their tour of Northern Ireland. Mac and I were left on rear party as part of a skeleton staff whose job it was to keep the barracks ticking over while they were away. The rear party consisted of soldiers who like myself were injured or due to leave the Army, but it also had a large body of the most useless wankers who were deemed unfit to even accompany them to Ireland. I could never understand why the Army tolerated them, instead of just booting them out altogether.

One of our tasks while on rear party was the cleaning and servicing of the Rapiers, which I enjoyed but it saddened me that I would never have the opportunity to fire it again. I thought back to our once-yearly firing camp up in the Outer Hebrides. The Rapier would be set up on the remote shoreline with numerous cables leading to a high-tech bunker, where every aspect of the operator and the Rapier's performance could be analysed for any mistakes or malfunctions. An aircraft would fly over the target zone towing a canister on a mile long cable and at a given moment the canister would release smoke enabling the Rapier operator to visually see it. There was always a host of electronic safety measures in force to prevent any risk to the aircraft itself. It was always a nerve wracking and exhilarating moment when pressing the fire button and feeling the missiles leaving the beams. Any soldier who managed to get the missile within a few feet of the canister would be credited with having hit the target because had it been a jetfighter it would have been much larger. Any soldier who was skilled or lucky enough to hit the canister itself would be given a tie and a crate of beer, the beer was our inspiration to do well. Having fired a missile the operator was then required to report to the SMIG for a debrief on his performance and this included watching a re-run on video. God help any operator who made a cock up. Occasionally a missile went rogue. This meant that once fired it would not accept the electronic commands from the Rapier, in effect it was out of control and the only course of action was to press the cancel switch thus exploding the missile. Fortunately only one missile I fired went rogue and my first indication that something was wrong was hearing the doors slam on the safety shelter behind me, as the lads dived for cover.

After skiving off from servicing the vehicles one day, Mac and I made our way back to the accommodation block to get a brew. As we walked into the corridor one of the lads who was also on rear party shouted to us.

"Scouse, Mac, come and see this on the telly." We walked into his room just in time see news pictures of a frenzied mob surrounding a car. I couldn't work out what was happening until one of the lads in the room told me it was the car of two British soldiers who had been cornered after driving into a funeral cortege. My blood ran cold as I watched the horrific events unfold before me. I felt revulsion and anger as I watched. There were five soldiers in the room that day and none of us had a dry eye. The rage I felt as I watched two fellow British soldiers being dragged from their car was like nothing I had felt before. They were being beaten to death in front of a watching world. I was in no doubt as to the fate of these poor men and sadly neither were they. This was a true picture of what the Republicans do best. Murdering innocent people. In their haste to kill they simply forgot that the world was watching. Every single person who was there that day from the people who watched and clapped to the scum who administered the coup de grace have blood on their hands and I hope their actions will live with them forever. I know in my own heart that I will always feel hatred for the people who carried out what I consider to be the worst crime I have ever had the misfortune to witness.

Mac and I stumbled back to our room feeling numb. I turned to Mac. "The sad thing is, the Americans who feel they are Irish because a great, great, great grandfather or whoever had emigrated to the States, will continue to put money in the tins for these bastards, with the misconception that they are supporting freedom fighters and not a bunch of thugs whose real occupations include murder, drugs, prostitution and racketeering."

The door swung open and one of the sergeants who was also on rear party walked into our room.

"Did you see it?" I asked him.

"Yes," he replied, "I hope they round up every bastard who took part, but on the subject of Northern Ireland," he said frowning, "Scouse, I am afraid you have got to go back out there."

"Is this some sort of sick joke?" I said thinking it was wind-up after what we had just seen on the telly.

"No," he replied, "I am deadly serious, but I haven't got the full details yet, its something to do with two lads you nicked for a burglary." I knew then that he was telling the truth.

"Fuck me," I said, "when do I have to go?"

"Err now." he said hardly able to contain his smile at my worried face. Mac burst out laughing,

"Scouse, they might decide to keep you there with 12 regiment."

I arrived in Belfast the following day via Heathrow airport and an overnight stay in an RAF camp after some confusion over my flight. I was met at the airport by a plain clothed soldier in an unmarked car. He stood out like a sore thumb and his guise wasn't fooling anyone, particularly the IRA.

"Welcome to sunny Belfast", he said laughing at his own joke as we got in to his car. He then went on to explain that I would be staying in a section of a barracks in East Belfast which was there specifically to accommodate soldiers who were court witnesses. Belfast reminded me of Liverpool, which is not far from where I live and as we chatted I completely forgot where I was until an Army patrol drove past us with gun-toting soldiers aboard.

On my arrival at the court witness section I was met by a very irate officer who demanded to know why I had not been there the day before. I explained to him that the travel arrangements were out of my hands and I had just followed orders and he calmed down. That afternoon John King arrived. John was a civilian, but had he not agreed to come over, the Army had said they would have subpoenaed him to court which meant he would have had to come in the end anyway. The officer tried the same routine 'of where the fuck have you been?' on John, but John politely reminded him that he was now talking to a civilian and to go and fuck off. I was envious that I wasn't in the position to do the same. That night John and I made for the bar and we both got well and truly pissed.

The following day the hangover stakes were being paid in full. I was taken to Londonderry in an unmarked car in the company of two plain clothed policemen and John was given an escort worthy of a visiting dignitary. The reason for this was simple, as a civilian his safety was very important but as a mere soldier I was more expendable. It had been almost a year since John and I had caught the two brothers burgling the garage, so the police gave us a quick refresher of our statements. Then we wandered off to the shop in the barracks for a brew, and who was standing behind the counter but Smiler? the choggy shop owner from Strabane. His face broke in to a huge grin when he saw John and me and I thought that he was happy at seeing two old faces from the past. Then he became more serious.

"You owe me money, you not pay your debts when you leave, you owe me for coffee and Kit Kats." Smiler was right,

I had sloped off without paying because I thought that I would never see him again.

I paid my debt to him and sat down with John who was laughing that Smiler had caught up with me.

"He's one tight-arsed bastard," I said to John, "it's been nearly a year since I saw him and he remembered that I owed him for a cup of coffee and a fucking Kit Kat. I will have the last laugh, watch."

"What are you going to do Scouse?" he asked curiously.

"Watch," I replied. "Smiler," I said calling him to the end of the counter. Smiler came over looking very apprehensive.

"What you want?" he asked keeping a safe distance.

"I just want a word, Smiler," I said trying to coax him over.

"No credit," he said, "you piss off last time, no pay."

"No, I don't want credit Smiler I want to tell you something," I said. But Smiler sensed that I was up to something and would not come near. I decided to play my ace card.

"Smiler, remember your camera?" I whispered across to him. Smiler's eyes widened and he was over to me in a second.

"You take it, you bastard!" he yelled.

"No, no, not me Smiler," I said, "but I can tell you who."

"Who take my camera?" Smiler begged.

"Promise you won't tell anyone if I tell you?" I asked him.

"No, me no tell," he said, "who take it."

"Promise," I said to Smiler, who was now hanging on my every word. I then whispered the name of a lazy bastard who had been with us in Strabane. I didn't think for one minute that Smiler's protests would get him anywhere but somebody was in for a lot of earache over Smiler's beloved camera.

At the last minute the two brothers changed their plea and admitted their guilt to burglary at the garage in Strabane. They really had no option as we had caught them bang to rights, but their little game of making the British taxpayer pay out lots of money had worked. Not only had the two brothers been given legal aid, but then there was the expense of flying John and I to Belfast and the security to escort John to the court. The only satisfaction was that both the brothers went to prison.

I arrived back in Germany a few days later to find Mac in a very pissed off mood and when I found out why I too was pissed off. He had been put on guard duty on a day on, day off basis, and the day off guard would be spent working on the vehicles. This meant working seven days a week and I was to join him. This was how we spent the summer of 1988. My knee problem was now causing me real problems and this wasn't helped by my standing on guard for hour after hour. I became bitter that the Army knew that I was in pain, but they still made me carry out guard duties. It was as though they were squeezing the last drop out of me before I left, broken and therefore of no further use. In the November Mac and I managed to get places on an Army pre-release course at Catterick garrison in Yorkshire.

The idea behind pre-release courses is to give soldiers who are leaving the Army, having served a minimum of six years, a skill to help them integrate back in to civilian life. That's the theory but the courses are limited and so is the amount of time spent on them. Most of the courses Mac and I had asked for were fully booked up from the beginning, all best places going to the senior ranks. In the end we were given a choice between painting and decorating or motor mechanics. I wasn't particularly keen on either, but along with Mac I decided to opt for the mechanics because my knowledge of engines only stretched to the servicing of our vehicles and I thought it may come in useful. The Staff Sergeant who was booking the course for us pointed out that it was only six weeks long and any soldier who thought that it would be of any use to him on leaving the Army was sadly mistaken. I had no intention of trying for a job in mechanics, but it made me realise that these courses were only a token gesture from the Army so they could say that they were helping soldiers back in to civilian life. Mac and I left Germany only too happy to escape from the continuous cycle of guard duties.

On the first day of the course all the assembled students including Mac and I were given a small test of ten questions to assess what mechanical knowledge we possessed. The instructor must have read the horror on the faces of Mac and I as he passed the test papers round the class, because he told us not to worry as it was a very simple test. Twenty pencil-biting minutes later he read out the results to the class. I had scored one point and Mac had done slightly better with two. I squirmed in my seat as the other students all laughed and to my annoyance the instructor joined in.

"Do you want to be on this course?" the instructor asked me nonchalantly as he looked at the students trying for another laugh at our expense.

"No I don't." I replied telling him the truth, "the only reason I am here is because I wanted to escape the guard duties in Germany and the only other course was painting and decorating." The room fell silent all the eyes were on me.

"And you?" the instructor said looking at Mac. "Same reason," he replied.

"Err, right go and see the RSM in charge of the course," he said "I don't want you here with that attitude." We made our way over to the RSM's office. "Well we are truly in the shit now," Mac said.

"I know Mac," I replied, "but I am past caring." And I was, the whole course was a charade and I knew that it would have no bearing on my life as a civilian. The one thing that would have made a difference was getting my knee treated when it mattered, but nothing had been done.

The instructor had already telephoned ahead of us because the RSM was waiting. "So you don't want to do the course!"

he screamed, "well get your fucking arses to Woolwich where they are waiting for you and when you get there you will start guard duties until you leave. Which is when?" he said pointing his pay stick at me.

"February sir," I told him.

"And you?" he said pointing at Mac. "February sir," Mac replied. "Well, good, because you can keep each other company," he shouted. "Now get the fuck out of here."

After trudging through snow Mac and I stood on Darlington station soaked through to the skin.

"Fuck this Ed, lets fuck off home for tonight and meet up tomorrow and then go to Woolwich," Mac suggested.

"I don't know Mac," I replied, "We're in enough shit already with that bastard back there."

"I know," he said, "but we can say the snow has delayed us."

"Fuck it okay," I relented. We made arrangements to meet, but once I reached home Mac phoned me to say his mother was ill and he didn't have to go back. I reported to Woolwich and received the same reception from the RSM, who accused me of trying to pull a fast one. I could not reason with him as what an RSM says goes and that is it. As punishment, I was put on guard duties until I was about to leave.

The day of my discharge arrived and I handed in my identity card. I picked up all the documents I needed, including my red book, which is the military equivalent of a curriculum vitae. The book described what a good soldier I had been and what a credit I would be to any future employer. It had been written by someone who didn't know me apart from snippets of information given by past troop commanders on my yearly assessments. It was all so matter-of-fact.

"Is there anything else?" asked the woman whose job it was to process soldiers leaving the Army.

"No," I replied.

"Well, thanks for everything you have done, whatever it

was," she said smiling. I nodded and she returned to her typing.

I began the walk back over to the transit accommodation to pick up my belongings which were contained in one single bag. Like a bolt of lightning it hit me that I no longer had a job or a home of my own and, to make things worse, I had an injury to my knee that was not improving. This time I did not have the option of re-enlisting. It was over for good. I knew it would not be like the last time I had left, I had to settle down.

The barracks where I had undergone my basic training in the flush of my youth was now host to another generation of eager young soldiers. All of them brimming with enthusiasm for the adventures that lay ahead. Nine years earlier I was of the same mind. I would have taken on the world single-handedly, but I never imagined for one moment that I would ever be called on to go to war for real. At the time I had dreams of myself strolling around the streets of Northern Ireland looking mean and hard as I suppose most young recruits do, but the real issues of Northern Ireland were lost on me then. I simply had no understanding of why the army was there in the first place. What made an impression on me were the television pictures of soldiers quelling riots, the dangers never crossed my mind.

People may think me stupid or gullible or both, but I never realised until the Falklands war that I had joined an organisation whose business was killing. In the beginning, what drew me in to the army careers office was to escape from the boring factory I was working in, but I also liked the idea of marching around in a red tunic and bearskin hat. All the posters on the walls of the careers office showing soldiers skiing and strolling along sun-soaked beaches appealed to me, I thought that it would be me in the posters. The army do not have a picture of a soldier with a sucking chest wound after a sniper attack in Belfast or lying in the gutter of a wet

Londonderry street with half his brains blow away. Images of soldiers screaming in fear while crouched in a muddy trench under attack from jet fighters will not attract the right sort of people into the army and yet that is the reality of it. I have seen man at his very worst killing each other.

All the books written about war can never portray the true horrors of it and that includes this one. When the Army doctor asked me if I was suffering with anything all those years ago I should have replied, "Yes, delusions of grandeur!"

Postscript

Since leaving the Army I have married and my wife Tricia and I have two children, Kristy and Nathan, and I couldn't be happier. However it has not been easy, because my knees never got better and I have undergone no fewer than seven operations. Sadly all have failed.

Though I have been out of the Army for some years now I still get moments when I miss it, but I also accept that it has changed very much. This change was most certainly brought about by the collapse of the Soviet Union which forced all the services to look at their roles in a politically changing world, none more so than the army and this has resulted in some dramatic changes. Some of the finest regiments have been amalgamated or disbanded altogether. Though it is sad it is also necessary, the Army must move with the times and be able to meet the changing demands.

Women are now playing a much bigger and far more important role than when I was serving. Without getting into the ethics of women going to war, I feel that if a woman is able to carry out her task as efficiently as a man, then I see no reason for not letting them do the job. After all it was a woman who sent the entire task force to war in 1982!

On the whole I have enjoyed writing this account of my life as a soldier, but sadly my father died before it came to fruition. I have tried to write this book from the heart and as accurately as possible. If any of my former colleagues perceive some of the events that I have described rather differently then I make no apologies, because this book describes the things I have seen through my eyes and my thoughts at the time.

In parts of this book I have had to alter names and omit some procedures for the security of the soldiers who are still serving.

Finally, as a man who has been to war I can say this: If the politicians could see the real horrors of war and look beyond the flag waving and celebrations of returning troops, if they could see the real misery of death and injury and the wrecked lives of all those involved, the disgusting savage acts men commit on each other in the name of war, then maybe there would be more effort to stop it happening at all.

Edward Denmark